821.7245
373
cop.1
T3
821.7245
373
cop.1
Fogle, R H
Idea of Coleridge's
criticism
1962
JUN 8
JUN 14
AUG 10
58741
63588
65309

# 9: PERSPECTIVES IN CRITICISM

PERSPECTIVES IN CRITICISM

1: *Elements of Critical Theory*

2: *The Disinherited of Art*

3: *Stream of Consciousness in the Modern Novel*

4: *The Poet in the Poem*

5: *Arthurian Triptych*

6: *The Brazilian Othello of Machado de Assis*

7: *The World of Jean Anouilh*

8: *A New Approach to Joyce*

9: *The Idea of Coleridge's Criticism*

9:

RICHARD HARTER FOGLE

# *The Idea of Coleridge's Criticism*



UNIVERSITY OF CALIFORNIA PRESS
*Berkeley and Los Angeles*
1962

*University of California Press*
*Berkeley and Los Angeles, California*
*Cambridge University Press*
*London, England*

LIBRARY OF CONGRESS CATALOG CARD NO. 62-10824
*Printed in the United States of America*
*Designed by Ward Ritchie*

*To Clarence DeWitt Thorpe, 1887-1959*

# *Preface*

Estimates of the value of Coleridge's criticism have varied widely, although few have questioned the fact of its influence. Among authoritative professional scholars René Wellek has been able to perceive in Coleridge's critical theory only eclecticism roving amid the ideas of transcendental Germans. With much respect for Coleridge's critical acumen and some regard for his consistency, Professor Wellek finds little originality in his thought. T. M. Raysor, the most notable editor of Coleridge's critical writings, has boundless admiration for his subject's psychological insights and his practical results, but he rejects Coleridge's system completely, dismissing its central theory of imagination with some self-restraint as "unfortunate." Raysor also has reservations about the appropriateness of the Coleridgean method to the drama, considering that Coleridge talks not about plays but about dramatic poetry. Something will be said later of this. Coleridge's most recent editor, Kathleen Coburn, is also noticeably cautious in her claims for him.

Fine general critics of our times, such as Eliot, Tate, and Ransom, have been repelled by Coleridge's romanticism. Desiring objective certainty and precision, and unalterably opposed to romantic monism and transcendentalism, they have taxed him with overphilosophizing, overpsychologizing, sentimentalizing, confusing, and in general muddying the waters of criticism and taste. The astringent F. R. Leavis remarked some years ago that the continued vogue of Coleridge was something of a critical scandal. Critics have been especially put off by what has seemed to them a confusion in Coleridge of subject and object, which Mr. Tate would no doubt set down ultimately to the noxious influence of Descartes. The objection is not new, as witness Carlyle, but it evidences either ignorance of or plain contempt for the very bases of Coleridge's system.

Others have been more favorable. It is not to the purpose here to speak at length of Coleridge's influence on criticism; indeed, I have little confidence that it could be reliably assessed. This influence, however, is undoubtedly both great and durable. One is surprised, for example, at its extent in the American golden age of the 1840's and 1850's, in Emerson, in Poe, in Hawthorne, in Melville, in Lowell, and in such contemporary powers as the now-forgotten E. P. Whipple. Later one comes upon its tracks in the delectable organicist narcissism of Henry James, a Coleridge sans philosophy, his critical eye turned inward upon the aesthetic vision in his own fiction. And in the critical renaissance of recent decades the place of Coleridge has been at the fore.

In 1948 Stanley Edgar Hyman stated in *The Armed Vision* (the title itself from the *Biographia Literaria*) that Coleridge is "the first really great modern critic," and that "the *Biographia Literaria* . . . is almost the bible of modern criticism. . . . He is . . . with the exception of Aristotle, certainly its most important progenitor." Modern critics and scholars such as James Baker (*The Sacred River,* 1958) have seen in Coleridge an early exponent of depth psychology, especially of the role of the unconscious and of dream in imaginative creation. Sir Herbert Read in particular has hailed him as a forerunner of surrealism and contemporary neoromanticism. Others have been fascinated by the possibilities of the Coleridgean "reconciliation of opposites" for contemporary doctrines of irony and paradox in poetic language. Correspondingly, and still more important, the modern critical dogma of identity of form and content, as propounded by Cleanth Brooks in such essays as "The Poem as Organism" and by Brooks and Warren in the now-famous *Understanding Poetry,* at the least received much support from Coleridge's theory of organic form. The degree of his influence would be impossible to calculate in the matter of organicism, for so many others might be pointed out as well: for example, Bosanquet, Bergson, and Croce. Yet Coleridge has been more accessible than these, and as a practical critic closer to the minds and hearts of his critical successors.

Above all, literary men have been heartened by his confidence in the meaning and the value of the language of the imagination. In a very large degree the formal literary criticism of the last two decades—one might almost add of the last two centuries—has waged continuous defensive warfare against the encroachments of science. Amid this battle the Coleridgean dictum, "Poetry, even that of the loftiest and, seemingly, that of the wildest odes, had a logic of its own, as severe as that of science; and more difficult, because more subtle, more complex, and dependent on more, and more fugitive causes," has been as exhilarating to litterateurs as was to Sydney the ballad of Chevy Chase, or Emerson's *American Scholar* to refractory young men in libraries. Coleridge's defense of the order of imagination against the usurping orders of logic and of scientific and recorded fact won a deep response, even from positivists like the early I. A. Richards; rejecting his metaphysics as ancestral moonshine, they wished perforce it had been truth, and succeeded in transforming it to a brand of moonshine rawer but more acceptable to their time, with the label of semantics.

Today Richards' and William Empson's provocative

studies of "the interinanimation of words" have told us what they can. Freudian, Neo-Freudian, and Jungian depth psychology has done its best and its worst, from Maud Bodkins' *Archetypal Patterns in Poetry* to Arthur Wormhoudt's *The Demon Lover*. Coleridgean dialectical exegesis, of the kind that he brought to bear in his Shakespearean criticism, and introduced to the schools by Cleanth Brooks, Robert Penn Warren, Robert Heilman, and others, has been assimilated and is no longer a horror and a delight. For the moment, indeed, Coleridge's criticism is neither a rallying point nor a position to be attacked, unless perhaps by Aristotelians—and they have had their full say on the iniquities of critical monism. There is, however, I am confident, a need for such a study as I here introduce: a study of Coleridge's criticism in itself, tentatively accepting the metaphysical assumptions on which it is based and focusing upon its central principles and inner relationships; endeavoring without direct regard for its external connections to the past and the present to see it as a whole, yet at the same time anxiously regardful of its permanent significance and its bearing upon practical criticism.

A straight view of Coleridge's criticism is hard to attain, from two serious hindrances: the nagging problem of his debt to the Germans and the incompleteness of his text. From De Quincey's attack in *Tait's Magazine* up to now there have always been scholars sincerely convinced that Coleridge owed an excessive debt to Kant, Schelling, the Schlegels, and others. He has had perhaps more defenders than attackers, yet the difficulty remains—for, once raised, it is not possible to settle it definitively. A recent University of Florida doctoral dissertation by Hardin McD. Goodman has considered it with magnificent thoroughness, examining the evidence for every German writer for whom influence on Coleridge has been alleged, and decisively rejecting the claim for any substantial indebtedness.

Yet even such a study as Goodman's can, in the complexity of the issues, neither provide absolute proof nor win conviction from opponents. Perhaps, once the question is opened, it is best simply to point, as does Alfred Harbage, to the enormous number of sources that Coleridge might well have had. Remarking upon the Germans' own debt to the English empiricists, Harbage shrewdly comments, "We can only conclude that a scion of stock so mixed, empirical English and empyreal German, must have had an identity of his own." We know, too, of some empyreal English in Coleridge's background in the seventeenth-century Cambridge Platonists; we could go on to the esoteric tradition in Swedenborg and Boehme; note an avowed debt to scholastic philosophy for such terms as "subject," "object," and "individuation"; find large infusions of Aristotle in Coleridge's poetics and dramatic theory; and conclude by noting his expressed allegiance to Plato in his later writing. What Coleridge took, we may well think, was in the public domain.

My own argument rests upon internal evidence: the self-consistency and the vitality of Coleridge's critical writing when it is deliberately confined to its own relationships. As organicist and transcendentalist Coleridge is indeed a child of his time, with a particular affinity for the great Germans. It does not necessarily follow that he derives from them. As a philosopher he does not rival Kant or Schelling in sustained and systematic thought because it is not at bottom his purpose to do so; he is a poet-philosopher-critic, and his total contribution, though greatest in criticism, is not separable into its component parts. Coleridge is a genuinely organic thinker, whose mind is a totality and who aims always at synthesis. He appears incomplete if any of his gifts are isolated from the rest: indecisive as an aesthetician, shadowily oracular as a philosopher, fragmentary as poet and critic.

The incompleteness of his critical texts of course

raises a formidable obstacle for the student. The *Biographia Literaria* itself is in a sense an accidental outgrowth of the publication of *Sybilline Leaves* and, ironically enough, the product of Coleridge at his nadir. The rest of his criticism is lecture notes, marginalia in books, reports of his conversation such as may be found in Crabb Robinson's *Reminiscences*, shorthand reports of his lectures by men of varying powers of comprehension, and, finally, passages in his relatively neglected letters and in journals only now publicly available through the industry of Miss Coburn, where an occasional critical nugget shines forth like a jewel in a manure pile. A critic of Coleridge's criticism often has to tread lightly, unsure how much weight it is safe to bring to bear.

Yet Coleridge is the greatest English romantic critic, and he stands among the greatest critics of all time. His work is a unique combination of theory and concrete practice, a building so spacious that many see only parts of it, and not the whole of his achievement. An inveterate synthesizer or syncretist, he presents a different aspect from different points of view. To the Aristotelian Ronald Salmon Crane, for example, he is basically a Platonist, in search of the one in the many. To some scholars of romanticism he shows kinship to Aristotle, as in his conception of symbol and of character as a fusion of the particular and the general. By some his thought is distrusted for its seeming eclecticism, whereas others are dismayed by a certain obsessive monotony in it. Crabb Robinson thought he detected in Coleridge the sterility of a closed mind, and complained in almost the same breath of his freedom in handling the great Germans; such talk, said Robinson, would not have been permitted in Germany.

But Coleridge was at once consistent and capable of growth, with fixed principles but limitless boundaries. It is the peculiarity of his thought to be at once organic and discursive, preoccupied with oneness and yet concerned to analyze. Thus comes about, as we shall later notice, his dual use of terms like "organic" and "imagination," which may stand according to their contexts either for the synthesis to be achieved or for the part to be synthesized by reconciliation with its opposite term. Coleridge is organicist, but he goes beyond organicism in its simple or extreme sense by trying to include within it the benefits of systematic and analytical thinking, as in his account of the mind as at once an organic unity and a hierarchy of faculties.

This study of Coleridge's criticism thus emphasizes its essential unity, an attribute difficult to demonstrate conclusively because of wide misunderstanding of his method and the incompleteness of his texts, and also because of persistent suspicions of his originality. The title, *The Idea of Coleridge's Criticism,* is at once an expression of confidence and of deference to doubters. *Idea,* in Coleridge's Platonic usage, is almost synonymous with *ideal,* the Platonic form of which the actual corpus of criticism is an imperfect and incomplete appearance, while yet implicating the perfect whole. So Eliot, himself drawing upon Coleridge, writes of *The Idea of a Christian Society.* Formally incomplete, Coleridge's criticism sketches the outlines of completeness nonetheless.

This large praise of him, in grain a romantic and in some ways a Platonist, should be sufficient warning to Aristotelians or proponents of criticism as a science. I sympathize with Coleridge's fundamental monism, and consider his critical scheme comprehensive enough to deal justly with the complexities both of literary history and of the individual work. I would maintain that pluralism is destructive of critical vitality and, conversely, that there can be no total objectivity in criticism (Coleridge's is a system of object as well as subject). Correspondingly, I would defend the tempered and complex monism of Coleridge against the absolute monism of much contemporary criticism. The conception of organic unity is unsatisfactory without the imaginative sense of the mind infused within the words of the literary object, and thus I distrust the attribution of complete autonomy, according to which a poem or a novel is literally possessed of its own life and unifying principle, independent of its creator.

All this is to avow great confidence in Coleridge himself, not merely as a historical example of romantic theory, or an interesting pioneer in the investigation of the unconscious mind, or a halfway house up the peak of modern organicism, but a critic sufficient in himself, of permanent value and enduring usefulness of application.

I owe grateful acknowledgments to Professors Thomas M. Raysor and René A. Wellek, who read part of this book in manuscript; to the John Simon Guggenheim Foundation and Henry Allen Moe for a fellowship and for gracious support and encouragement in general; to the Tulane University Council on Research for generous and repeated help in grants; to the libraries of Tulane University, Cornell University, and the University of North Carolina; to Francis E. Mineka, Meyer H. Abrams, and Floyd Stovall for various kindnesses; and to Sarah Kost, whose services in typing my manuscript have gone far beyond the requirements of duty. Especially I owe gratitude to the late Clarence DeWitt Thorpe for his critical insight, his fine scholarship, and his unfailing friendship.

R. H. F.

# *Contents*

# 1

## *Critical Principles*

THE CRITICISM of Coleridge is uniquely comprehensive.[1] Although it commences with the idea of unity and makes unity its chief preoccupation, it allows for particularity. It intends to be systematic, yet sufficiently flexible to deal with even the minutest problems of style; grounded upon synthesis, it yet does not evade analysis. It possesses a metaphysic and an aesthetic, which it however applies successfully in practical criticism.[2]

The chief emphasis of Coleridge's criticism is psychological. Poetic creation is the fullest activity of the mind, and to understand a literary work one must look to the qualities of the mind behind it. But this is Coleridge's emphasis, not the whole of his search. The relationships of his position reach far. His psychology is organically one with his metaphysics, which assume an ultimate reality and an attempt to explain it. Mental faculties like reason, understanding, and imagination are not only components of mind, but organs of knowledge as well. Coleridge's aesthetics is psychological insofar as it is concerned with effect, the mind's reaction to an aesthetic object; it describes by introspection the pleasure that the object can give. This pleasure, however, is the subjective counterpart of a beauty that objectively exists. The difference between Coleridge's psychological criticism and such contemporary psychological criticism as I. A. Richards' earlier work is almost antipodal.[3]

Coleridge's criticism is based upon the idea of unity as the necessary principle of reality. His system would assign to the individual literary work its appropriate place in the total structure of literature. This structure or cosmos is an organic whole, but it is composed of literary genres, ranged tacitly according to their values. These genres are for the most part named from the traditional Aristotelian system; Coleridge uses the familiar terms of epic, tragedy, comedy, pastoral, lyric, without enumerating them or arranging them with formal completeness.[4] His conception of genre is nevertheless distinct from Aristotle's, and differs still more widely from the genre-thinking of neoclassical critics.

In the *Poetics* Aristotle conceives of epic and tragedy as forms absolute in themselves, which can be fully realized by the poet and objectively described by the critic. The progress of such genres is in part, but only in part, historical. Tragedy evolves in time, under historical conditions, gradually growing in fullness and complexity, until it has reached perfection; at this point, as it ceases its development, it ceases its connection with history. The neoclassical critic takes up the genre where Aristotle leaves off. An epic or a tragedy is to him a determined and static object, composed of distinct parts in a mechanical arrangement and governed by fixed rules. Thus in planning *The Rape of the Lock* Pope could commence with an established formula for the "heroicomical," and with appropriate models in poems like Boileau's "Lutrin" and Garth's "Dispensary."

Coleridge differs from Aristotle and all neoclassics in his larger allowance for individuality. Every work is unique, and subject only to laws proper to itself, so that no predetermined code can wholly deal with it. This recognition of the claims of the unique individual does not, however, lead to critical anarchy; it merely points to a fact which consideration shows to be self-evident. Every literary object must be unique, or must possess aspects that are unique. This does not prevent rational consideration and classification of it. At the same time it is natural that system-seeking criticism should avoid this obvious yet difficult truth. Coleridge, as he seeks balance [5] everywhere, seeks here the perfect balance between universal and particular, and tries to describe his object as individual, in kind and in its universal significance.

In this balance the theory of genres is a keystone. It is too little noticed how often the words "class," "kind," "species," and "genus" appear in Coleridge's criticism,[6] and how often he insists upon the necessity of determining the genre of a work before passing judgment upon it, or, as he would say, the necessity of distinguishing kind before degree. This caution is intended not to exclude judgment, but to direct it. A swan or an eagle should not be exposed to criteria formed from the observation of doves.

> We call, for we see and feel, the swan and the dove both transcendently beautiful. As absurd as it would be to institute a comparison between their separate claims to beauty from any abstract rule common to both, without reference to the life and being of the animals themselves—say rather if, having first seen the dove, we abstracted its outlines, gave them a false generalization, called them principle or ideal of bird-beauty and then proceeded to criticize the swan or the eagle—not less absurd is it to pass judgement on the works of a poet on the mere ground that they have been called by the same class-name with the works of other poets of other times and circumstances, or any ground indeed save that of their inappropriateness to their own end or being, their want of significance, as symbol and physiognomy.[7]

This passage emphasizes the individuality of the swan, or the eagle, or the poet. The swan, however, is itself a class, and the attack is not upon generalization but upon false generalization and abstraction.[8]

Coleridge's value on this subject lies not in an articulated system but in his perception that kind and individual coexist. For him a literary genre will depend: (1) upon general human nature, in which it is grounded; (2) upon time, place, and circumstances—as these, for example, account in part for the difference between Greek tragedy and the "romantic drama" of Shakespeare; (3) more vitally upon the mental faculties that determine the genre in their scope, arrangement, and relative dignity; (4) correspondingly, upon the depth and breadth of reality which the genre is capable of imitating; and (5) upon the specific literary effect that is intended. Above all, genre in Coleridge is "motivated." Superficial form acquires meaning and life from the intellectual, emotional, and artistic reasons for its existence.

Coleridge's conception of genre is based upon the method of the reconciliation of opposites, which embodies the characteristic method of his thought. Kind can be reconciled on the one hand with individuality, on the other with the universal. By careful distinction definition can be reconciled with the judgment of value, since kind is distinguished from degree. The reconciliation of opposites, indeed, is the Archimedes lever of Coleridge's criticism. His procedure and his terminology are dialectical or "polar."[9] Reality is always organic unity or wholeness, but this reality can only be discursively revealed as two,[10] in the form of polar opposites reconciled, or of centripetal and centrifugal forces in equilibrium. In aesthetics this principle involves the full acceptance of the doctrine of organic unity of form and content, but at the same time it preserves their distinctness as concepts, for without their twoness organic unity would be structureless and unintelligible.

The reconciliation of opposites is possible under two conditions. The first requirement is the conception of an agent or, as Coleridge sometimes says, a copula that is capable of unifying opposing forces. The second is that the opposing forces themselves should be such as can be reconciled. Opposites do not reconcile themselves, but are reconciled by a sufficient power; on the other hand, there are limits to the unifying capacity of the copula. Consequently the oppositions in a poem must not be taken as somehow reconciled because they lie adjacent to each other. For Coleridge true opposites must be essential each to the other. For example, he sees the vital principle of Scott's novels in their fundamental opposition of conservation and reform:

> The essential wisdom and happiness of the subject consists in this,—that the contest between the loyalists and their opponents can never be *obsolete,* for it is the contest between the two great moving principles of social humanity; religious adherence to the past and the ancient, the desire and the admiration of permanence, on the one hand; and the passion for increase of knowledge, for truth, as the offspring of reason—in short, the mighty instincts of *progression* and *free agency,* on the other. In all subjects of deep lasting interest, you will detect a struggle between two opposites, two polar forces, both of which are alike necessary to our human well-being.[11]

The reconciliation of opposites is the organizing principle of Coleridge's psychology. The imagination is the copula of the mind, which reconciles its active and its passive powers. "There are evidently two powers at work, which relatively to each other are active and passive; and this is not possible without an intermediary faculty, which is at once both active and passive.

(In philosophical language, we must denominate this intermediate faculty in all its degrees and determinations, the IMAGINATION. . . .)"[12] Imagination mediates between reason and understanding, "which relatively to each other are active and passive." Reason enables man to apprehend truths beyond the reach of the senses. It is immediate in action and indemonstrable by discursive argument, since its grounds are in itself. Itself the starting point of thought, nothing in the mind can explain it. From the reason comes our idea of God, our idea of spirit, our idea of unity. Its existence, so to speak, rests only upon the affirmation "it is," since the mind knows it and its ideas, just as a man must say, "I am."[13] Reason's opposite, the understanding (our ordinary "reason"), is the discursive intelligence, the faculty by which we deal with phenomena. The understanding organizes the evidence of the senses for logical and practical use; it enables us to survive in and even to manage the material world. It is the conceiving, generalizing, and abstracting power by which we compare and classify; it is the faculty of scientific method. The understanding cannot perceive individuals or things-in-themselves, but only

> that inanimate cold world allowed
> To the poor loveless ever-anxious crowd.[14]

It sees things as dead ("all objects [as objects] are essentially fixed and dead"),[15] and can conceive mechanical structures only.

It is vital to remember that the faculties of Coleridge's psychology are, as he says, distinct but not separate.

> The office of philosophical *disquisition* consists in just distinction; while it is the privilege of the philosopher to preserve himself constantly aware, that distinction is not division. In order to obtain adequate notions of any truth, we must intellectually separate its distinguishable parts; and this is the technical process of philosophy. But having

> done so, we must then restore them in our conceptions to the unity, in which they actually co-exist; and this is the result of philosophy.[16]

The mind in its workings is one: the faculties are not definite, not objects of the senses. To know the mind we must analyze it, yet realize the limitations of analysis.

Therefore in conceiving the faculties as separate, as we must do in order to understand them, we are setting up necessary fictions. Reason, for instance, is impossible without the faculty of understanding, except in the mind of a madman. Thus Don Quixote is mad: "Don Quixote grows at length to be a man out of his wits; his understanding is deranged. . . . He becomes a substantial living allegory, or personification of the reason and the moral sense, divested of the judgment and the understanding." [17] The faculties develop different relationships according to need and point of view. Thus reason and understanding are logical opposites, which may be taken as opposing equals. Reason, however, is a more comprehensive faculty which transcends the understanding. So also imagination changes according to need and emphasis. Although reason is the highest faculty, yet as the reconciler of reason and understanding imagination is generally more important; it is the agent that "brings the whole soul of man into activity." [18] Coleridge distinguishes between the primary imagination common to all, which is the instrument of his psychology and his philosophy, and the secondary or specifically poetic imagination, which is the instrument of his criticism.

Oppositions form the framework of Coleridge's criticism. These oppositions are either deduced from the primary distinction of reason and understanding or they are at any rate analogous to this distinction. Imagination is opposed to fancy, genius to talent, organism to mechanism, symbol to allegory, imitation to copy. As with the faculties of the mind, however, the relations of these pairs are complex. In this simplest relationship they are antithetical and therefore equal, yet in each pairing the first term represents a more inclusive content, a more complex unity, a fuller harmony, an intenser activity.[19] Consequently it indicates superiority, but the distinction is rather of more and less than of good and bad. Fancy, for example, is inferior to imagination. It arranges but cannot, like imagination, re-create and transform its materials. Its relationships are merely superficial and mechanical, but in its sphere it is valuable nevertheless. Without fancy imagination would suffer, both in definition and as a critical tool. Organic unity is likewise superior to but not independent of mechanical unity, which is as the skeleton to the body.

The well-known discussion of imagination in chapter xiv of the *Biographia Literaria* is a microcosm of Coleridge's entire critical system.[20] The imagination brings into play the whole soul of man, reconciling image and idea, the concrete and the abstract, emotion and judgment, enthusiasm and good sense, sameness and difference. It would be almost impossible to overemphasize the importance in Coleridge's thought of the unifying, vitalizing, organic force of imagination. Without the conception of its cohesive power his critical system can be seen in parts and fragments only. Difficult to grasp, and liable to be dismissed as chimerical, the notion of the unifying power could yet be justified, if for no other reason, by its central position in all Coleridge's thinking, whether literary, scientific, psychological, metaphysical, or theological.

The primary imagination performs the creative act of consciousness itself. The secondary or poetic imagination "dissolves, diffuses, and dissipates in order to recreate" the material furnished by the primary imagination, and, a matter briefly stated but fundamental to its use in artistic creation, it coexists with the conscious will. It idealizes or at least struggles to idealize.[21] It seeks to create, whereas the fancy arranges materials already given. The imagination is a higher faculty akin to the reason, but unlike the reason it images the ideal, and unlike the understanding it idealizes rather than abstracts from images. To the imagination nature is real and living. As copula and mediator between reason and understanding it partakes of both and yet is neither.[22] The end of reason is spiritual truth, and the end of understanding is the demonstrable truth of science; the end of imagination is the beauty of truth, by means of which truth is accessible to the spirit.

To Coleridge organic unity is a means of describing both the imaginative work and the imaginative mind that creates it.[23] Its symbol is the living plant or tree, whose life is not in roots, or trunk, or branches, or leaves, but pervades them all and is paradoxically "all in each." [24] Organic unity therefore involves the mystery of life itself as the unifying agent. "The organic form . . . is innate; it shapes as it develops itself from within, and the fulness of its development is one and the same with the perfection of its outward form. Such [as] is the life, such [is] the form." [25] The principle of organic unity also includes:

1) The mysterious process of growth, in which the parts develop simultaneously from a seed in which the matured organism is already contained.

2) The inseparability of form from content. Mechanical unity is predetermined and superimposed from without. The potter molds the clay by a process not inherent in the material itself. In organic unity the formal principle lies within, and the outlines of the formed object are the outer limits of its creative impulse.

3) The inseparability of the part from the whole. An organic part is irreplaceable. This has a direct bearing upon our conception of the interrelationships of a literary work, and therefore of our methods of analyzing it and our criteria for judging it.

4) Great complexity of process. The copresence of conscious and unconscious, discursive and immediate, willed and spontaneous.

The idea of organic unity is wonderfully appropriate to imaginative art, in its complex intermingling of conscious and unconscious, of premeditated and spontaneous elements. Organic unity, however, implies the impossibility of complete discursive description. A fine poem is like a living being. Its totality is indefinable; it can be grasped only in an imaginative insight not wholly reducible to rational expression.[26] Thus recent critics have come to say that a good poem is "inexhaustible to contemplation."

Some of the attractions of organic unity are dangerous. Its proper application to literature is metaphorical, and one must bear in mind that metaphor implies not only likeness but difference. The organic unity of art is not the organic unity of nature; it is a product of conscious will and intelligent effort. Critics have sometimes gone wrong by taking their own figures of speech too literally; a poem is not a plant or a tree. Coleridge did not confuse likeness with complete identity.[27] Such a confusion frequently leads to a notion of a mystical whole which is insusceptible of analysis. But of course analysis is an indispensable way to knowledge, and few have analyzed more elaborately than Coleridge, who maintained that the ability to distinguish was the hallmark of the philosopher. Criticism, he said, like philosophy, must be based upon principles, must be as systematic as possible in relation to its proper means and ends. "Till the reviewers support their decisions by reference to fixed canons of criticism, previously established and deduced from the nature of man; reflecting minds will pronounce it arrogance in them thus to announce themselves to men of letters, as the guides of their taste and judgement."[28]

The idea of organic unity does not, in short, excuse us from the duty of using our minds. Wrongly taken, the great truth that form and content are inseparable can lead us into obscurantism. We may, for example, suppose that this truth forbids us to distinguish between form and content, so that critical discourse becomes impossible. On the other hand, we may be led to discuss either form or content exclusively, under the mistaken impression that we are discussing both. Organic unity furnishes, however, a means of demonstrating that analysis, though indispensable, is not enough. Literary criticism must begin with an act of the imagination, only after which analysis becomes possible. Just as Coleridge reconciles that analytical conception of distinct mental faculties with the organic conception of the unified mind, so he reconciles perception of the literary whole and its parts.

Through organic unity Coleridge is able to deal with the basic contradiction of neoclassicism. The great English neoclassical critics—Dryden, Addison, Pope, and Johnson—were all plagued by the discrepancy between the literary object and the critical weapons at their disposal. Dryden "loved" Shakespeare, but was really much happier with Ben Jonson. Pope was quite willing to allow that there are "nameless graces," but they had to remain nameless, beyond the reach of art and judgment. Despite, too, the many excellences of Johnson's Preface to Shakespeare, it is finally unsatisfactory. Johnson is honest and resolute, but his conclusions are all unresolved antitheses. The gaps between art and nature, between genius and judgment, remain unclosed. Shakespeare, having defied the rules of rational criticism, is mysteriously the more successful for his lawlessness.

The neoclassical contradiction arises from a method of antithetical thinking, embodied in the sentence structures of Pope's poetry and Johnson's prose,[29] which leaves its oppositions wholly separated. Coleridge did not reject the method, but transcended it. He considered that nature and art, genius and judgment are opposites but not disparates; that they are different aspects of the same whole, and can be reconciled if we conceive a unifying force. Shakespeare's "judgment is equal to his genius" because one is necessary to the other. Genius cannot be realized unless judgment directs it; and without genius judgment is empty. Correspondingly, the greater the genius the greater the judgment required to control it. Shakespeare is not lawless, although not susceptible to the predetermined rules of neoclassical criticism. On the contrary he is the embodiment of law, but this law is organic and inner; it cannot be imposed mechanically from without.[30]

Thus Coleridge banished Shakespeare, the untutored child of nature who violated the laws of composition but still mysteriously succeeded. The bad neoclassical critic, like the ineffable Rymer, applies his rules to everything, and makes an ass of himself in his laughter at Shakespeare's asininity. The good neoclassical critic, like Dryden or Johnson, is aware of a large uncharted area which he vaguely denominates inspiration or nature. Coleridge endeavors to map out a wider territory, but still without pushing the method of discursive analysis further than it can properly go.

Coleridge's method of analysis may be deduced from his doctrine of organic unity. He looks first for an informing principle, correspondent to the all-pervading life of an organic body: the "germ" that contains potentially the completed form, as the acorn contains the oak. This principle or germ appears intelligibly (since reality is intelligible only in the form of polar opposites) as an opposition; in drama, for example, it appears as a dislocation in the hero's mind which is the source of the drama's action. This dislocation is psychological, a disproportion of mental faculties. Coleridge speaks of "Shakespeare's mode of conceiving characters out of his own intellectual and moral faculties, by conceiving any one intellectual or moral faculty in morbid excess and then placing himself, thus mutilated and diseased, under given circumstances."[31] The phrase "intellectual and moral" indicates, however, that psychology is not to be separated from reality.

Thus in *Hamlet* the tragic action arises from an imbalance between the mind of the hero and external reality. Hamlet is a giant of intellect who lacks the will to act. Satisfied with the rich reality of his inward life —"his thoughts, images, and fancy [being] more vivid than his perceptions"[32]—the outer world is unreal to him, dim like the pictures which remain a moment before closed eyes. Clearly discerning the moral necessity for acting, he cannot act. His mind is a richly figured curtain when he needs a window. *Don Quixote* is also determined by a mental disequilibrium. The hero is a symbol of pure reason. Don Quixote perceives spiritual truth, but does not understand actuality. Giants and windmills are the same to him. Sancho Panza, on the other hand, represents common sense without reason (he is thus fitly a servant). The two combined would make one perfect soul, but as separate individuals they cannot unite. The movement of the novel is the movement of their relation: first one dominates, then the other, and only at the end do they achieve equilibrium.[33]

For Coleridge the inner struggle of the individual mind was doubtless the most interesting of all conflicts. The issues of the struggle, however, were always to be of wide interest, and the individual was not the only informing principle he envisaged. In *Romeo and Juliet* the action springs from family life which, unopposed by other forces, evolves in the play into irrational because ungrounded strife. Sheer pride of family, unmodified by any broader morality, leads to disorder. From this initial distortion comes the opposition of the old, the agents of the family principle, and the young, who are the victims of it. From it springs also the distinguishing character of the play—precipitancy. Acting as they do, unguided by sufficient cause, the old are arbitrary, hasty, and capricious, and in reaction the young are forced to be so too. Montague and Capulet resort to arms in an instant; old Capulet rages at the mere idea of opposition; Romeo destroys Juliet and himself by unneeded haste, which yet arises naturally from circumstances for which not he but his elders are to blame. The *feeling* of the play also stems organically from its central principle. It is pervasively youthful and springlike, in keeping with our sympathies, which are on the side of the young.[34]

Coleridge requires that the life principle of a literary work shall possess universality and permanence. It may be predominantly though not exclusively either intellectual or moral. It may be loftily metaphysical so long as it is grounded in universal human thought and feeling. Genres have their guiding principles as well as individual works, although they are more generalized; epic always shows the predominance of fate over free will, whereas tragedy permits the will to conquer in defeat. Romantic drama exemplifies the triumph of the imagination over time and space, under the opposing necessity of essential probability. Thus time and space in *The Tempest* have no importance, and supernatural mingle with real characters; yet Ariel and Caliban must be natural in their supernaturalness, and Ferdinand and Miranda must be typical, recognizable young lovers.[35]

There are three questions to ask about the possibilities of applying Coleridge's critical method to concrete practice. First, how is the value of the life principle to be tested? This principle constitutes the thesis of the critique, which consequently stands or falls by it. The answer is that we test it first by our intuitive sense of its rightness, and go on to consider its consistency discursively in detail. To understand any object we consider its consistency discursively in detail. To understand any object we assume its unity. We assume further that this unity can be intelligibly (though incompletely) described, and we define the best principle of unity as that which will explain all possible parts, all possible difficulties, without contradictions or with the minimum of contradictions, and with the maximum of fullness. Our description will then be accurate but still incomplete, for the total unity of a work is an organic unity of which a logical account will serve but as a part for the whole. Thus Coleridge remarks that *Hamlet* is the work "in the *intuition* and *exposition* of which I first made my turn for philosophical criticism . . . noticed." [36] This is his critical process in a phrase. The work is intuited, and then expounded.

The true unity, says Coleridge of the famous three unities, is unity of action or of interest. This alone is genuinely organic and universal of application. (Unity of interest, which Coleridge draws from Schlegel, should in his thinking be interpreted either as "capable of interesting" or, more discursively, as representing that interest aroused in reader or spectator by the organic unity that is its origin.)

> Instead of unity of action I should great[ly] prefer the more appropriate tho' scholastic and uncouth words—homogeneity, proportionateness, and totality of interest. The distinction, or rather the essential difference, betwixt the shaping skill of mechanical talent, and the creative, productive life-power of inspired genius: In the former each part [is] separately conceived and then by a succeeding act put together. . . . Whence [arises] the harmony that strikes us in the wildest natural landscapes—in the relative shapes of rocks, the harmony of colors in the heath, ferns, and lichens, the leaves of the beech and oak, the stems and rich choc[ol]ate branches of the birch and other mountain trees, varying from verging autumn to returning spring—compared with the visual effect

> from the greater number of artificial plantations? The former are effected by a single energy, modified *ab intra* in each component part.[37]

Unity, then, is realized in harmony and relationship —"in the relative shapes of rocks, the harmony of colors." Coleridge's practical criticism is constantly occupied with this concept of harmonious relationship, in varying shades and gradations. Thus the servants introduce the theme of *Romeo and Juliet:* "The domestic tale begins with domestic[s], that have so little to do that they are under the necessity of letting the superfluity of sensorial power fly off thro' the escape-valve of wit-combats and quarreling with weapons of sharper edge, all in humble imitation of their masters."[38] Likewise Coleridge's fine account of the first scene in *Hamlet* treats it as a microcosm of structural harmony, containing gradation, transition, development, contrast, and variety of intensity and pace. A whole in itself, it is a part of the larger whole of *Hamlet.* "The armour, the dead silence, the watchfulness that first interrupts it, the welcome relief of guard, the cold, the broken expressions as of a man's compelled attention to bodily feelings allowed no man—all excellently accord with and prepare for the after gradual rise into tragedy. . . ."[39] As to the consistency and staying power of Coleridge's critical method, it is enough to point out that he expounds much of *Hamlet* scene by scene in accordance with his principle of organization. He is able to interpret the various characters in their relations to Hamlet, to show that all the action stems from Hamlet, and to explain the style by his conception of Hamlet, as in the diction of the gravediggers' scene: "The contrast between the clowns and Hamlet as two extremes—the [clowns'] mockery of logic, the traditional wit valued like truth for its antiquity, and treasured up, like a tune, for use."[40]

The second question to be asked of Coleridge's criticism, considering that its method is dialectic, is: Does it confuse a work of art with a philosophical argument? This may be answered summarily, at least for the moment. The ultimate ends of philosophy and art are doubtless the same, but their immediate ends are different. Art is under the necessity of providing pleasure by means of unity of interest. In abstract terms the theme of *Hamlet* is the danger of thought uncompleted by action, but the play embodies rather than proves the theme. Coleridge remarks that "the general idea is all that can be required from the poet, not a scholastic logical consistency in all the parts so as to meet metaphysical objections." [41] The relationships are imaginative and representational, not strictly logical.

The third question is: Will not Coleridge's critical system, like other systems, bind us down to an inflexible procedure? If we accept the principle of organic unity, shall we then be betrayed into using a mechanical method? The way of escape, however, is in the principle itself, which lies within the particular work and must be found there, not imposed from without. This principle, the organic unity of interest, will be clearest seen by the clearest sight, and best defined by the best intelligence. The criticism that depends upon it must be analytical, but the parts it analyzes have first to be accounted for in their proportion and mode of arrangement. A critic must be methodical to be intelligible, but the method is not the criticism. It should be such as will permit the critic to apply his particular gifts to the fullest advantage; without a method he cannot apply them at all.

# 2

## *Coleridge on Organic Unity: Life*

THE BASIS FOR Coleridge's theory of organic unity is his idea of life itself, which is most systematically developed in his *Theory of Life*.[1] The *Theory of Life* is similar in purpose to an unpublished fragment on "the law of bicentrality," and like it is completely nonliterary in content.[2] Like it, however, it is highly significant as an instance of the homogeneity of Coleridge's thinking in quite diverse fields of knowledge, and it presents exact and detailed parallels with his literary criticism. I shall therefore summarize the *Theory of Life* at length as a foundation for discussing Coleridge's theory of organic unity.

Life defined absolutely, says Coleridge, is "the principle of unity in *multeity*, as far as the former, the unity to wit, is produced *ab intra*." We may note that he has recourse immediately to a reconciliation of opposites. But "*eminently* (*sensu eminenti*), I define life as *the principle of individuation*, or the power which unites a given *all* into a *whole* that is presupposed by all its parts.[3] The link that combines the two, and acts throughout both, will, of course, be defined by the *tendency to individuation*." The same process of reasoning continues in the distinction of absolute and "eminent" definitions, and their reconciliation by the copula ("link") of "the tendency to individuation." It is evident from the beginning, also, that organic unity and the reconciliation of opposites are essentially identical, since the unity can be conceived only as a reconciliation.[4]

The tendency to individuation is manifested in nature in "an ascending series of intermediate classes, and of analogous gradations in each class." From the lowest and simplest forms of life to the highest and most complex the powers peculiar to life are homogeneous, "degrees and different dignities of one and the same tendency." Life is latent even in the elementary powers of mechanism when they are considered "as qualitative and actually synthetic," and these lower powers are assimilated, not merely employed, by the higher.[5]

The definition of the kind, says Coleridge, is in its fullest sense the definition of the highest degree of that kind (an important observation for practical criticism, as will be seen later). If, then,

> life, in general, be defined *vis ab intra, cujus proprium est coadunare plura in rem unicam, quantum est res unica;* the unity will be more intense in proportion as it constitutes each particular thing a whole of itself; and yet more, again, in proportion to the number and interdependence of the parts, which it unites as a whole. But a whole composed, *ab intra,* of different parts, so far interdependent that each is reciprocally means and end, is an individual, and the individuality is most intense where the greatest dependence of the parts on the whole is combined with the greatest dependence of the whole on its parts.

The highest degree of life is the intensest unity, which is also the intensest individuality; the greatest wholeness consists with the highest development of the parts. The idea of wholeness, however, is dominant, as always with Coleridge, for the dependence of the parts on the whole is absolute.[6]

As all life has a tendency to individuation, its forms may be classified according to the degrees of individuation of which they are capable. Gold and "other noble metals" compose the lowest class; of the two counteracting tendencies of nature, detachment and attachment, they have least of the former, most of the latter. This class is "the form of unity with the least degree of tendency to individuation." The next step is the crystal, a union not only of powers but of parts, and therefore not merely a unity but a totality. The third step is sedimentary rock, as residue and product of vegetable and animal life, and conversely as manifestations of the tendency of the life of nature toward the vegetable and the animal. These constitute the fourth and last step. In the lowest forms of the vegetable and animal world "we perceive totality dawning into *individuation,* while in man, as the highest of the class, the individuality is not only perfected in its corporeal sense, but begins a new series beyond the appropriate limits of physiology." The tendency to individuation is the common characteristic of all these classes, while their degrees, both of intensity and extension, form the species, and their ranks in the scale of ascent and expansion.[7]

The tendency to individuate, however, is inconceivable without the opposing power to connect, and this polarity, or the essential dualism of nature, is the most general law of life. Polarity arises out of the productive (vital, not abstract nor mechanical) unity of nature, and still tends to reaffirm it, "either as equilibrium, indifference, or identity."

> Life . . . we consider as the copula, or the unity of thesis and antithesis, position and counterposition,—Life itself being the positive of both; as on the other hand, the two counterpoints are the necessary conditions of the *manifestations* of Life.

> . . . Thus, in the identity of the two counter-powers, Life *sub*sists; in their strife it *con*sists: and in their reconciliation it at once dies and is born again into a new form, either falling back into the life of the whole, or starting anew in the process of individuation.[8]

The law of polarity arises from the vital, not the mechanical, unity of nature, for in mechanism "the result is the exact sum of the component qualities, as in arithmetical addition. This is the philosophy of Death, and only of a dead nature can it hold good. In Life, and in the view of a vital philosophy, the two component counter-powers actually interpenetrate each other, and generate a higher third, including both the former."[9] Thus, according to this method of reasoning, the magnetic, electric, and chemical powers, the last and highest powers of inorganic nature, are in the vitalist view metamorphosed into reproduction, irritability, and sensibility.[10] These relationships are not analogies. Life is not like magnetism, or like electricity, but the animal life of man is the identity of all three. The lower terms are assimilated into the higher. "Analogy implies a difference in sort, and not merely in degree; and it is the sameness of the end, with the difference of the means, which constitutes analogy."[11] The lungs of a monkey are not analogous, as are the gills of a fish, to the lungs of a man.[12]

Coleridge continues by denying that he identifies life with magnetism, electricity, or chemical affinity as such, and the denial leads him to repudiate further the notion that life can be conceived "under the image of a subtile fluid or substance" which penetrates all bodies. The vital principle does not supervene upon an organized body, "something in the same manner as the steam becomes the *mechanic* power of the steam-engine, in *consequence* of its compression by the steam-engine; or as the breeze that murmurs indistinguishably in the forest becomes the element, the substratum, of melody in the Aeolian harp, and of consummate harmony in the organ." Such a view would assume that organization could preëxist without the organizer, the life principle. "Now this hypothesis is as directly opposed to my view as supervention is to evolution, inasmuch as I hold the organized body itself, in all its marvelous contexture, to be the PRODUCT and representant of the power which is here supposed to have supervened to it." This intimate and evolutionary relationship of life to organization, with the life, however, always the prior conception, is exemplified in the processes of nature throughout all its degrees to its consummation in the human body, which illustrate "at once the unceasing *polarity of life, as the form of its process, and its tendency to progressive individuation as the law of its direction.*" [13] The idea of evolution is now more heavily emphasized.

To begin at the beginning of the evolution of life, in order to account for form one must first imagine a state antecedent to form. Milton was wrong in describing a chaos of heterogeneous substances: "The requisite and only serviceable fiction . . . is the representation of CHAOS as one vast homogeneous drop," as "an appropriate symbol of the great fundamental truth that all things spring from, and subsist in, the endless strife between indifference and difference. The whole history of Nature is comprised in the specification of the transitional states from one to the other." [14] The progress of Nature is better represented by the rungs of a ladder than by the links of a chain, and she expands by concentric circles. This raises the fundamental problem how to reconcile her continuity with the conception of the interspaces between her forms or classes. But this contradiction is explained away by polarity itself, with its laws of attraction and repulsion, expansion and contraction. ". . . the whole *actual* life of Nature originates in the existence, and consists in the perpetual

reconciliation, and as perpetual res
mary contradiction, of which univ
result and the exponent." Nature
and reciprocally contracts, on the pr
*pour mieux sauter*. Her "tranquil depositio
prepared, as it were, the fulcrum of her after-
and "from this, her first, and in part *irrevocable*, se
contraction we find, in each ensuing production, more and more tendency to independent existence . . . first of vegetable and then of animal life."[15] This discussion vitally concerns Coleridge's consistent reconciliation of unity with partness, his conception of distinctness without separation. The process of evolution continues to its climax, man, with whom, it will be recalled, the series of physiology ends and a new series begins: ". . . that last work, in which Nature did not assist as handmaid under the eye of her sovereign Master, who made Man in his own image, by superadding self-consciousness with self-government, and breathed into him a living soul." Man is the culmination of the tendency to individuation, the consummate organization of the life principle. "In Man the centripetal and individualizing tendency of all Nature is itself concentred and individualized—he is a revelation of Nature! . . . Nor does the form of polarity, which has accompanied the law of individuation up to its whole ascent, desert it here. As the height, so the depth. The intensities must be at once opposite and equal. As the liberty, so must be the reverence for law."[16]

A number of points about *Theory of Life* need at this juncture to be made or remade as especially important for subsequent discussion:[17]

1) Life and organization or organized body are inseparable, but life is always the anterior conception, the subject, the agent. Thus depending upon the point of view life is either above or within the body it informs; or more properly it is *both* above and within it.

2) The definition of life as unity in multeity is essentially the same as Coleridge's definitions of beauty and of the poetic imagination.

3) Correspondingly, the account of individuation in its highest degree is also Coleridge's account in other contexts of ideal aesthetic and poetic structure.

4) The organic unity that is individuation is purposefully evolutionary.

5) This organic unity is dialectically reconciled with an orderly (though dynamic) cosmos composed of ranks and degrees, and degree is in turn reconciled with kind,[18] as continuity is reconciled with distinctness by assimilation (expansion) and gradation. Summary only inadequately suggests Coleridge's achievement in embodying this process in the movement of the essay itself.

6) Coleridge's "theory of life" must cope with the problems of two major gaps: the space between inorganic and organic nature, and the space between the natural and the supernatural orders in man. He deals with these major difficulties by the preconceived idea of unity, which is the point or peak of view that he assumes. And thus he denies that he is using mere analogy; he employs instead the concepts of assimilation, expansion, and elevation.

From his point of view the inorganic is a part that can be assimilated into the whole of the organic process (as, in other fields, fancy to imagination, and understanding to reason), and the principles of attraction and repulsion, contraction and expansion, and evolution (which is also elevation) are adequate to explain both the continuity of the process of individuation and the distinctness of each particular class. Each recoils yet advances, contracts in order to expand, and sinks to rise; it withdraws into itself to gather its forces in preparation for a further development of life. Now, as regards the possibility of an orderly evolution from natural to supernatural life, Coleridge specifically limits himself to physical life alone;[19] but the inferences of his method are irresistible. For if, as he says, man is a composition of natural and supernatural elements, as sedimentary rock is a composition of inorganic and organic elements, and as according to the logic of his argument each class both contracts into its individuality and in the same act prepares for a further elevation and expansion, then it would follow that natural and spiritual life are distinct but continuous, different degrees of the same existence. The statement that "in man, as the highest of the class, the individuality is not only perfected in its corporeal sense, but begins *a new series* [italics mine] beyond the appropriate limits of physiology"[20] seems highly significant. The phrase "a new series" strongly suggests a further orderly ascent from man to angels and archangels, thrones, principalities, and powers, as in the imagined hierarchies of *The Ancient Mariner.* And as Coleridge has consistently argued in *Theory of Life* that the complex can be successfully approached, if not explained, by orderly ascent from its lower and simpler elements, as life by magnetism, electricity, and "chemical affinity," so it would seem that natural life can shadow forth the supernatural.

*II*

Coleridge had spoken more explicitly on this all-important issue of the continuity of physical and spiritual life in a letter of 1806 to Thomas Clarkson, in which he strove to explain his beliefs about God and the soul. His reasoning, which commences with God, postulates an orderly and full progression of Being from the lowest to the highest:

> What is (that is, what can we congruously conceive of) the Soul?—
>
> As the Father by and for the Word, and with and thro' the Holy Spirit has given to all possible

Existences all susceptible perfection, it is in the highest degree probable that all things, susceptible of Progression, are progressive; and as Intelligence involves the notion of *order,* it follows necessarily, that as we can have no notion of desirable Progression . . . but what supposes a growth of consciousness—or the image of that incommunicable attribute of self-comprehension, to which all creatures make approaches. . . . Now from those Possibilities, which exist only in the consciousness of others . . . to the highest consciousness short of Deity there must subsist infinite orderly degrees—1. those who exist to themselves only in moments, and whose continuousness exists in higher minds. 2. those who are conscious of *a* continuousness, but not only not of their whole continuousness, but who do not make that consciousness of *a* continuousness an object of a secondary consciousness—i.e. who are not endued with reflex Faculties. 3. Those who tho' not conscious of the whole of their continuousness, are yet both conscious of *a* continuousness, & make that the object of a reflex consciousness—And of this third Class the Species are infinite; and the first or lowest, as far as we know, is Man, or the human Soul. . . . Hence . . . I can define the human Soul to be that class of Being, as far as we are permitted to know, the first and lowest of that Class, which is endued with a reflex consciousness of it's own continuousness, and the great end and purpose of all it's energies & sufferings is the growth of that reflex consciousness: that class of Being too, in which the Individual is capable of being itself contemplated as a Species of itself, namely, by it's conscious continuousness moving on in an unbroken Line, while at the same time the whole Species is capable of being regarded as one Individual.[21]

Thus physical and spiritual life, though distinct, are yet unified in one great pattern or series. As we have seen, the lower entity is the representative type of the higher, as it partakes in its lesser degree of the same reality. "What the Spirit of God *is*, and what the Soul *is*," writes Coleridge to Clarkson, "I dare not suppose myself capable of conceiving: according to my religious and philosophical creed they are *known* by those, to whom they are revealed, even (tho' in a higher and deeper degree) as color (blue for instance); or motion; or the difference between the Spirals of the Hop-plant and the Scarlet Bean." [22] Correspondingly Coleridge's allusions to life treat it indifferently as animal or as spiritual, and depending upon the context either as immanent or as transcendent, within or above, or both; for, according to the point of view, it may be the body informed by it, or the informing principle, or the reconciliation of the two, the higher power always informing the lower. Life as subject is always conceived as anterior to life as object, or organization.

Coleridge, then, conceives of life as physical and natural growth and continuity in the plant, and tree, and stream, and in the living body; as social growth in the "body politic" of the organic state; [23] as psychological growth in the evolution of the human mind from the senses; as the imaginative growth of a work of art from its seed or germ of an idea; and as spiritual growth from the germ of the practical reason or will.[24] In each instance the principle of life is "*ab intra*." But life also comes from above, as light, or more specifically as the sun,[25] and its ultimate source is God, the great I Am,[26] the supreme Self-consciousness. Each living thing is in its degree the reconciliation of these two principles, or more properly these two opposite directions of the same principle.

For Coleridge the living structure or organic unity is dynamic; it is an act or a process that evolves in orderly progression toward an end preconceived, unconsciously or consciously according to its degree in the scheme of Being. As act or process it must be realized or embodied—it is a real thing, but is never wholly objective or self-contained. As a thing it will possess distinct parts which are, however, inseparably interrelated; as a process it will evolve in distinct steps, which are reconciled with its continuity by the notion of gradation, and by action and reaction. As thing or body it will reconcile matter with spirit, and substance with form. Ideally speaking, a natural scene, a social structure, the human mind, a poem, a painting, or a musical composition is an organic unity.

The organic unity of a natural scene will serve best for concrete illustration, and Coleridge's conversation poem, "This Lime-Tree Bower My Prison," is a notable instance of his theory in its representation of nature, and in its proper unity as a structure:

> Well, they are gone, and here I must remain,
> This lime-tree bower my prison! I have lost
> Beauties and feelings, such as would have been
> Most sweet to my remembrance even when age
> Had dimm'd mine eyes to blindness! [Ll. 1–5.]

Life springs up in the apparent spontaneity and immediacy of the opening lines, which catch as it were a link of an unbroken and continuous chain of thought, and the words of the poem are in effect coinstantaneous with the mental experience they embody. The poem is a vital movement of the poet's mind, an inner experience, its parts and relationships the living growths of the thought and the feeling which are its seed. Feeling is the prime impulse and mover: feeling not as the negation of intellect but as that which sets intellect in motion.[27] Nor does the primacy of the feeling imply incoherence, the absence of intelligible parts to the poem. Its effect is rather to subtilize their interrelationships, to disguise variety in unity. We are inclined to pass over transitions which of themselves are striking.

The movement of the poem is circular—a snake with its tail in its mouth, in Coleridge's words [28]—or perhaps more properly cyclical or cumulative. The poet remains in his bower, but he undergoes a complete experience. It is a reconciliation of opposites, with thesis, antithesis, and synthesis. He is regretful at his loss of a valued opportunity; his regret is momentarily forgotten in its opposite, his imaginative participation in his friends' enjoyment; the two extremes are reconciled, as he returns to himself and the limited but genuine value of the lime-tree bower. This reconciliation takes on body and life from the natural scenes of its setting, the extremes of a "roaring dell" and its opposite the "many-steepled tract magnificent," reconciled as it were in the mingled richness and delicacy of the bower.

They, meanwhile,
Friends, whom I never more may meet again,
On springy heath, along the hill-top edge,
Wander in gladness, and wind down, perchance,
To that still roaring dell, of which I told;
The roaring dell, o'erwooded, narrow, deep,
And only speckled by the mid-day sun;
Where its slim trunk the ash from rock to rock
Flings arching like a bridge;—that branchless ash,
Unsunn'd and damp, whose few poor yellow leaves
Ne'er tremble in the gale, yet tremble still,
Fann'd by the water-fall! and there my friends
Behold the dark green file of long lank weeds,
That all at once (a most fantastic sight!)
Still nod and drip beneath the dripping edge
Of the blue clay-stone.

Now, my friends emerge

Beneath the wide wide Heaven—and view
again
The many-steepled tract magnificent
Of hilly fields and meadows, and the sea,
With some fair bark, perhaps, whose sails light
up
The slip of smooth clear blue betwixt two Isles
Of purple shadow! Yes! they wander on
In gladness all; but thou, methinks, most glad,
My gentle-hearted Charles! for thou hast
pined
And hungered after Nature, many a year,
In the great City pent, winning thy way
With sad yet patient soul, through evil and
pain
And strange calamity! Ah! slowly sink
Behind the western ridge, thou glorious Sun!
Shine in the slant beams of the sinking orb,
Ye purple heath-flowers! richlier burn, ye
clouds!
Live in the yellow light, ye distant groves!
And kindle, thou blue ocean! So my friend
Struck with deep joy may stand, as I have
stood,
Silent with swimming sense; yea, gazing
round
On the wide landscape, gaze till all doth seem
Less gross than bodily; and of such hues
As veil the Almighty Spirit, when yet he makes
Spirits perceive his presence. [Ll. 5–43.]

The two scenes are direct opposites: the dell is deprivation, the landscape fullness. The dell is obscure, "o'erwooded, narrow, deep," and almost hidden from the eye of God ("And only speckled by the mid-day sun"). The single ash tree is "branchless," "Unsunn'd and damp," with merely a "few poor yellow leaves." The other growth is the file of "long lank weeds." The motion is an involuntary reflex of dull half-life; the leaves tremble, the weeds nod and drip. The colors are correspondingly lifeless and dull in the pale yellow of the leaves, the dark green of the weeds, the opaque blue of the "clay-stone." From this deep, narrow, almost lightless dell the friends *emerge* "Beneath the wide wide Heaven," and view, in Coleridge's orotund Miltonic phrase, "The many-steepled tract magnificent," the variety and profusion of whose "hilly fields and meadows" is further enriched by the prospect of the sea, animated perhaps by "some fair bark," its sail a subsidiary light which vivifies "The slip of smooth clear blue betwixt two Isles / Of purple shadow." Colors—clear blue, deep purple shadow, the brighter purple of the "heath-flowers"—are distinguished, modulated, and finally blended and fused by the yellow light of the setting sun, visible in itself and also the informing principle that unifies and permeates the whole wide landscape. In the climactic passage the landscape dissolves into pure unity in variety, pure embodiment, as if it were a revelation of the essence of God to high though lesser spirits.

This is the antithetical relationship of the dell and the landscape, but the scenes are connected in other ways. The element of contrast that is involved in antithesis implies subordination also.[29] The dell clearly is used to enhance the effect of the landscape, and thus to form a step in a ladder of upward progression to the climax of the imagined revelation of Godhead. To antithesis, then, one must add subordination, with the further consequence of gradation and progression.

There remain two problems of the dell and the landscape: the copula or organic unity in which the two become one, and conversely their individualities, in which they are wholes in themselves. Their vital connection is manifested by the interfusion in each passage of the same life in images of motion, feeling, and energy. Even the dell is animated: the ash flings its slim trunk from rock to rock, and the waterfall imparts its life to the leaves which tremble and to the weeds which nod and drip. So in the landscape a higher life from the sun shines, burns, and kindles, till at the climax, as the watcher stands "'Silent with swimming sense," it might be said that the light of sense goes out, but with a flash that lights the invisible world.

Likewise the two scenes in their different degrees share a common richness and fullness. The dell has its own completeness and structure in its ash-tree bridge, and its subtle reciprocities and reconciliations in the ever-still but ever-moving waterfall, the leaves that "Ne'er tremble in the gale, yet tremble still," the weeds that are caught in a frozen stillness of simultaneous motion—indeed, in the interesting ambiguity of the "still roaring dell" itself. The opposing landscape, as has been noticed, possesses variety of contour, form, and color, all interpenetrated by the unifying power of the sun which, like Coleridge's own contemplative act, makes things "less gross than bodily."

A delight
Comes sudden on my heart, and I am glad
As I myself were there! Nor in this bower,
This little lime-tree bower, have I not mark'd
Much that has sooth'd me. Pale beneath the
blaze
Hung the transparent foliage; and I watch'd
Some broad and sunny leaf, and lov'd to see
The shadow of the leaf and stem above
Dappling its sunshine! And that walnut-tree
Was richly ting'd, and a deep radiance lay
Full on the ancient ivy, which usurps
Those fronting elms, and now, with blackest
mass
Makes their dark branches gleam a lighter
hue
Through the late twilight. . . . [Ll. 43–56.]

The transition from the landscape to the lime-tree bower is gently modulated, from the "delight" of the vicarious experience to the soothing quality of the actual. In the broader reconciliation of the poem the two earlier scenes are interfused in the imagery of the bower, which, relatively speaking, possesses the straitness and the pallor, the general privation imputed to the dell, but is also endowed with the rich light and variety of the landscape, with an added complexity in the subtle interplay of light and shadow, the mingled harmony and distinctness of object and hue, exemplified by the delicate dappling of one leaf upon another, the relativity of the dark elm branches to the darker masses of ivy, and the modulating influence of the gradual movement of time and the afternoon sun. Compared to the landscape scene the bower is subdued, as color is not directly named and as it is associated with the coming-on of darkness. Within it the mingled discontent and imaginative joy of the poet are steadied, tranquilized, and reconciled. Symbolically "the last rook" flying home at sundown establishes another connection, with the sun and with the friend, Charles Lamb, who, Coleridge imagines, must have seen the bird as it "cross'd the mighty Orb's dilated glory," or "flew creeking o'er thy head." Lamb is used both to contrast and to unify. His strange misfortunes and his long sojourn in the City enhance the pleasure attributed to him in the life of nature, while his broad human sympathy verifies the conclusion already suggested by the all-unifying sun, that "No sound is dissonant that tells of Life."

# 3

## *Coleridge on Organic Unity: Beauty*

ORGANIC UNITY, as we have seen, manifests itself in the reconciliation of opposites, which Coleridge variously describes as equilibrium, balance, equipoise, polarity, harmony, mesothesis, interpenetration, identity, indifference, fusion, blend, coexistence, consubstantiation, coördination, and intermediation—to list some representative terms. Relations between opposites vary on the one hand between the extremes of absolute likeness and absolute diversity, on the other between absolute predominance and absolute equality, according with the principles of degree and gradation implicit in his theory of life. The elements to be reconciled must, however, be opposites and not contraries. Sweet and sour are opposites, but sweet and bitter are contraries and irreconcilable, different not merely in degree but absolutely in kind. Thus in Coleridge's critical dichotomies the organic and the mechanical would be opposites, and possible to reconcile, although on one plane of discourse they operate as contraries. The mechanical, from the point of view of unity, is a part or a lower aspect of the organic and is transformed or assimilated into it, whereas from the point of view of diversity it is its contrary. "Imitation" and "copy" would also be contraries, for a copy is not merely partial and insufficient but positively bad from its application to a wrong purpose in its claims to be a work of art. As the distinction of imitation and copy belongs exclusively to the discourse of art and criticism, the terms themselves would have to be altered to permit of reconciliation, and this is not true of the more inclusive organic-mechanical opposition.

All reality manifests itself as opposition, and the primal opposition is between subject and object. Coleridge's terms are consequently prevailingly subjective or objective according to the direction of his approach, from the agency that unifies to the elements that are unified, from the whole to the part, or from the unity that permeates or interpenetrates multeity to the balance or harmony in which this unity is actually revealed. There is no inconsistency in Coleridge's "Aesthetical Essays," in which the end of his inquiry is the beauty of the aesthetic object. These have been taxed with confusion of subject with object, or with departure from Coleridge's customary position. At times they have been preferred to his other criticism by virtue of an imputed superiority in objectiveness. They are, however, not different, nor superior, nor inferior. They present a characteristically Coleridgean conclusion arrived at by a characteristically Coleridgean method: specifically, a reconciliation of the concepts of life and beauty by a reconciliation of subject and object. The argument, apparently fragmentary, is really an orderly evolution. Consequently it seems permissible, as well as convenient for my purpose, to treat as one the four essays, "On the Principles of Genial Criticism," "Fragment of an Essay on Taste," "Fragment of an Essay on Beauty," and "On Poesy or Art."

Almost at the outset of these essays Coleridge's excellent editor Shawcross objects to his definition of the common principle of the fine arts because "it has the defect of being at once subjective and objective, i.e. based both upon the motive of the artist and the nature of his creation."[1] "The common essence of all consists in the excitement of emotion for the immediate purpose of pleasure through the medium of beauty"[2] is the definition in question. If the passage is separated from its context the objection undoubtedly has merit; one is startled to find that a "common essence" is "the excitement of emotion." The formula has been prepared for, however, by a preceding sentence, "The same spirit speaks to the mind through different senses by manifestations of itself, appropriate to each," in which Coleridge gives notice of it, and its place in the general discourse is further indicated by the explanation that "Philosophy [unlike mathematics] . . . concludes with the definition: it is the result, the compendium, the remembrancer of all the preceding facts and inferences. Whenever, therefore, it appears in the front, it ought to be considered as a faint outline, which answers all its intended purposes, if only it circumscribe the subject, and direct the reader's anticipation toward the one road, on which he is to travel."[3] Shawcross actually points out this road to the reader by suggesting in his note that "This definition of art should be re-examined in the light of Coleridge's subsequent explanations," but he unaccountably declines to follow it himself. The definition would be defective if it could be shown that (1) it dealt inadequately with the "subject," (2) it dealt inadequately with the "object," or (3) it confused rather than reconciled the two. Viewed in context it is free of these faults.

It will be noticed in the definition of the fine arts that the subjective "emotion" and "pleasure" are counterparts of the objective "beauty" they reflect. This can be true because the aesthetic response in the mind is itself "objective" in the sense that it conforms to universal law. Coleridge's request that "the reader would steadily look into his own mind to know whether the principles stated are ideally true"[4] presupposes that these principles are universal both inwardly and outwardly. He remarks that "the Apollo Belvedere is not beautiful because it pleases, but it pleases us because it is beautiful." Thus the beauty and the pleasure are both objective in the sense that they are real and conform to intelligible laws. Taste, therefore, is not relative but absolute, and aesthetic tastes differ not in kind but merely in degree. Distinguishing between the beautiful and the agreeable, Coleridge urges,

> let not these distinctions be charged on the writer, as obscurity and needless subtlety; for it is in the nature of all disquisitions on matters of taste, that the reasoner must appeal for his very premises to facts of feeling and of inner sense, which all men do not possess, and which many, who do possess and even act upon them, yet have never reflectively adverted to, have never made them objects of a full and distinct consciousness. The geometrician refers to certain figures in space, and to the power of describing certain lines, which are intuitive to all men, as men; and therefore his demonstrations are throughout *compulsory*. The moralist and the philosophic critic lay claim to no *positive,* but only to a *conditional* necessity. It is not necessary, that A or B should judge *at all* concerning poetry; but if he does, in order to a just taste, such and such faculties *must have* been developed in his mind. . . .[5] But more especially on the essential difference of the beautiful and the agreeable, rests fundamentally the whole question . . . whether the noblest productions of the human genius (such as the Iliad, the works of Shakespeare and Milton, the Pantheon, Raphael's Gallery, and Michael Angelo's Sistine Chapel, the Venus de Medici and the Apollo Belvedere . . .) delight us merely by chance, from accidents of local associations—in short, please us because they please us (in which case it would be impossible either to praise or to condemn any man's

> taste, however opposite to our own . . .); or whether there exists in the constitution of the human soul a sense, and a regulative principle, which indeed may be stifled and latent in some, and be perverted and denaturalized in others, yet is nevertheless universal in a given state of intellectual and moral culture; which is independent of local and temporary circumstances, and dependent only on the degree in which the faculties of the mind are developed; and which, consequently, it is our duty to cultivate and improve, as soon as the sense of its actual existence dawns upon us.[6]

Taste, then, is innate; it lays claim to a contingent necessity only, but is essentially universal ("stifled and latent in some, perverted and denaturalized in others"); tastes differ in degree and not in kind, and are therefore, as *taste*, susceptible of rational discussion and explanation. "Whatever can be brought to the test of general principles presupposes a distinct origin from these pleasures and tastes, which, for the wisest purposes, are made to depend on local and transitory fashions, accidental associations, and the peculiarities of individual temperament: to all which the philosopher, equally with the well-bred man of the world, applies the old adage, *de gustibus non est disputandum.* Be it, however, observed that 'de gustibus' is by no means the same as 'de gustu.'"[7]

Significantly, taste is defined in terms almost identical with those elsewhere used of imagination, as "the intermediate faculty which connects the active with the passive powers of our nature, the intellect with the senses; and its appointed function is to elevate the *images* of the latter, while it realizes the ideas of the former."[8] Like the imagination it is a mediator between active and passive, subject and object. Coleridge remarks that its metaphorical derivation from one of "the mixed senses," which blend the perception with the sense of the object,[9] "will teach us to expect in its metaphorical use a certain reference of any given *object* to *our own being* [italics mine], and not merely a distinct notion of the object as in itself, or in its independent properties."[10] Thus the "Beautiful arises from the perceived harmony of an object . . . with the inborn and constitutive rules of the judgement and imagination."[11]

The reality of taste is contingent upon the reality of externality or nature, and its essential oneness with the mind, which must also be real. The notion of the naturally agreeable, as green is naturally agreeable to the eye, involves "a pre-established harmony between the organs and their appointed objects,"[12] and "the first species of the Agreeable can alone be a compound part of the beautiful, that namely which is naturally consonant with our senses by the pre-established harmony between nature and the human mind."[13] "As light to the eye, even such is beauty to the mind, which cannot but have complacency in whatever is perceived as preconfigured to its living faculties."[14] And thus in taste is involved the definition of the fine arts, "the chief and discriminative purpose of which it is to gratify the taste,—that is, not merely to connect, but to combine and unite, a sense of immediate pleasure in ourselves with the perception of external arrangement."[15] Correspondingly art "is the mediatress between, and reconciler of, nature and man,"[16] and commences with "the effect produced by the congruity of the animal impression with the reflective powers of the mind; so that not the thing re-presented, but that which is re-presented by the thing, shall be the source of the pleasure."[17] "Of all we see, hear, feel and touch," Coleridge says, "the substance is and must be in ourselves; and therefore there is no alternative in reason between the dreary (and thank heaven! almost impossible) belief that everything around us is but a phantom, or that the life which is in us is in them likewise."[18]

All genuine art is a reconciliation of subject and object. There is a great difference between true imitation of nature and false imitation, or copy; copy deals with the object alone, the superficial form, and is thus dead, as in waxwork figures of men and women; imitation reconciles the subject and the object, as in a good portrait, and consequently lives.

> In all imitation two elements must coexist, and not only coexist, but must be perceived as coexisting. These two constituent elements are likeness and unlikeness, or sameness and difference, and in all genuine creations of art there must be a union of these disparates. The artist may take his point of view where he pleases, provided that the desired effect be perceptibly produced,—that there be likeness in the difference, difference in the likeness, and a reconcilement of both in one.[19]

The artist errs in copying "the mere nature, the *natura naturata*," the given form. "Believe me, you must master the essence, the *natura naturans,* which presupposes a bond between nature in the higher sense and the soul of man."[20]

The conception of beauty develops in an organic evolution throughout the "Aesthetical Essays." Whether Coleridge actually saw his way clearly at every step it is useless to inquire; at times he seems to waver, to go sideways or even backward. Yet his over-all treatment of beauty has the classic movement of his reconciliations. It commences with a unity that is dissolved into diversity, and reconciled to unity again—but a higher, more complex unity, evolved from progression. The problem is to reconcile beauty with life or its counterpart organic unity, without destroying the distinctions that must exist between them. So, though with a shift in emphasis, the basic definitions are almost identical. The "absolute" definition of life is unity in multeity, whereas the "most general definition of beauty" is "Multeity in Unity."[21] Beauty is then distinguished from life as different in kind (as in imagination-fancy and organic-mechanical) by abstract definition, as must be done to avoid confusing the terms. But there are degrees of beauty, ranging from simple to complex, from low to high, until, as distinguished from its abstract definition in kind, beauty in its fullness and height is reconciled and identified with life as organic unity. As in the *Theory of Life* the lower forms and powers of nature shadow forth the higher, and life progresses in unbroken continuity, so Coleridge moves in the "Aesthetical Essays" from the crystal, the triangle, "first-born of beauty," and the wheel, to the full-fledged work of art like "Raphael's admirable Galatea," which reconciles the shapely, without life in itself, and the vital. The earlier definitions and illustrations are parts of the whole, or the skeleton to the body of beauty.

Beauty is multeity in unity, and the triangle is its first and simplest symbol.[22] It is "that in which the *many*, still seen as many, becomes one,"[23] and thus, as with the tendency to individuation in life, the fullest possible reconciliation between partness and wholeness.[24] Beauty is independent of association and external reference; it is harmony, "and subsists only in composition." It is distinct from the merely agreeable, but the naturally agreeable, "that namely which is naturally consonant with our senses by the pre-established harmony between nature and the human mind,"[25] is a component part of the beautiful. At this stage of the argument "the shapely (i.e. *formosus*) joined with the naturally agreeable constitutes what, speaking accurately, we mean by the word beautiful (i.e. *pulcher*)."[26]

This is beauty, however, as perceived merely through "the highest impressions of sense." There is a higher and more complex version of the beautiful which arises from the addition of life and free will. A fuller beauty answers the fuller activity of mind. "What then will be the result, when the Beautiful, arising from regular form, is so modified by the perception of life and spontaneous action, so that the latter only shall be the object of our conscious *perception,* while the former merely acts, and yet does effectively act, on our feelings?"[27] This result is illustrated by Raphael's Galatea. It is "the balance, the perfect reconciliation, effected between these two conflicting principles of the FREE LIFE, and of the confining FORM! How entirely is the stiffness that would have resulted from the obvious regularity of the latter, *fused* and (if I may hazard so bold a metaphor) almost *volatilized* by the interpenetration and electrical flashes of the former."[28]

Coleridge does not pursue the problem of vital beauty at this point; indeed, he apologizes for "anticipating materials which rather belong to a more advanced stage of the argument." He continues instead with his careful distinction between the beautiful and the agreeable. The naturally agreeable "cannot, indeed, with strict propriety, be called beautiful, exclusive of its relations, but one among the component parts of beauty, in whatever instance it is susceptible of existing as a part of a whole."[29] Since beauty is harmony, and subsists in composition, a single tone or color may be agreeable but not beautiful. Individual qualities may aid negatively, however: "Something there must be to realize the form, something in and by which the *forma informans* reveals itself: and these [i.e., smoothness, and richness of sound], less than any that could be substituted, and in the least possible degree obscure the idea, of which they (composed into outline and surface) are the symbol."[30]

Beauty is now redefined in a reconciliation of subject and object: "The sense of beauty subsists in simultaneous intuition of the relation of parts, each to each, and of all to a whole: exciting an immediate and absolute complacency, without intervenience, therefore, of any interest, sensual or intellectual."[31] Beauty differs from the good, which is above it, and the agreeable, which is below it, in its immediacy; both the good and the agreeable "act on the WILL, and excite a desire for the actual existence of the image or idea contemplated: while the sense of beauty rests gratified in the mere contemplation or intuition."[32] Being immediate and self-sufficient, beauty represents the subjection of matter to spirit so as to be transformed to symbol, and the highest degree of beauty is that in which the most obstacles to manifestation have been overcome.

Beauty is not merely functional; it does not "originate in our perception of the fitness of the means to the end."[33] This issue is interesting in connection with modern theories of organic unity, in literature, in art, and in architecture. Functionalism involves a kind of monism, an absolute subjection of means to ends and part to whole, which Coleridge would never have sanctioned. And for Coleridge the idea of beauty has an absolute reality which is foreign to functionalism. Likewise beauty does not "depend on a law of Proportion," "were it only that proportion implies the perception of the coincidence of quantities with a pre-established rule of measurement, and is therefore always accompanied with an act of discursive thought." Predetermined parts would involve a merely mechanical unity: dead, literal copy rather than imitation. The long neck of the swan is brought in evidence. "We ask not what proportion the neck bears to the body;—through all the changes of graceful motion it brings itself into unity, as an harmonious part of an harmonious whole. The very word 'part' imperfectly conveys what we see and feel; for the moment we look at it in division, the charm ceases."[34]

In his fullest definition of beauty Coleridge reveals his method by adding the element of degree explicitly to kind, against a background of evolution in orderly steps:

> It is, in the abstract, the unity of the manifold, the coalescence of the diverse; in the concrete, it

> is the union of the shapely (*formosum*) with the vital. In the dead organic it depends on regularity of form, the first and lowest species of which is the triangle with all its modifications, as in crystals, architecture, & c.; in the living organic it is not mere regularity of form, which would produce a sense of formality; neither is it subservient to anything beside itself.[35]

Here is kind and degree; the abstract and the fuller concrete; the oppositions (the shapely and the vital, the dead and the living organic), and the assumptions of unity and evolution by orderly degree which are the agents of their reconciliation.

As beauty does not reside with a preëstablished rule of measurement, so the artist errs in copying "the *natura naturata*," mere objective nature. "If he proceeds only from a given form, which is supposed to answer to the notion of beauty, what an emptiness, what an unreality there always is in his productions, as in Cipriani's pictures! Believe me, you must master the essence, the *natura naturans*, which presupposes a bond between nature in the highest sense and the soul of man."[36] Coleridge continues to develop both his complex idea of beauty and the scheme of reality evolving by degree which is its rationale:

> In the objects of nature are presented, as in a mirror, all the possible elements, steps, and processes of intellect antecedent to consciousness, and therefore to the full development of the intelligential act; and man's mind is the very focus of all the rays of intellect which are scattered throughout the images of nature. Now so to place these images, totalized, and fitted to the limits of the human mind, as to elicit form, and to superinduce upon, the forms themselves the moral reflections to which they approximate, to make the external internal, the internal external, to make nature thought, and thought nature,—this is the

> mystery of genius in the Fine Arts. Dare I add that the genius must act on the feeling, that body is but a striving to become mind,—that it is mind in its essence![37]

Art imitates nature, but only the beautiful in nature, the essence, the *natura naturans,* which is objectified in the ideal symbol. The steps by which the objects of nature ascend toward "the full development of the intelligential act" correspond with the ascending and expanding degrees of beauty toward its highest development in the pure symbol, in which matter and spirit, mind and nature, are perfectly reconciled. It is said that "in every work of art there is a reconcilement of the external with the internal; the conscious is so impressed on the unconscious as to appear in it. . . ." Now, "He who combines the two is the man of genius; and for that reason he must partake of both. Hence there is in genius itself an unconscious activity; nay, that is the genius in the man of genius."[38] This relationship between the conscious and the unconscious in the man of genius corresponds precisely with the relationship between regular form and "life and free-will" in the beautiful. "What then will be the result, when the Beautiful, arising from regular form, is so modified by the perception of life and spontaneous action, as that the latter only shall be the object of our conscious *perception,* while the former merely acts, and yet does effectively act, on our feelings?"[39] Regular form is the basis of beauty, as the unconscious is the genius in the man of genius, but they are the abstractions that define the kind, not the vital forms in which beauty and genius are manifested. Or otherwise, they are the foundations of the total structure, and different from it only in degree and development. "And each thing that only appears to live has also its possible position of relation to life, as nature herself testifies, who where she cannot be, prophesies her being in the crystalized metal, or the inhaling plant."[40]

The statement "that body is but a striving to become mind" anticipates the climactic identification of beauty and life or organic unity in their final causes or, in Coleridge's more usual wording, their ultimate ends. Of symbol he had earlier agreed with the "Mystics" in declaring "*that* the *most* beautiful, where the most obstacles to a full manifestation have been most perfectly overcome." [41] Novelty or variety is usually defined in the same terms as beauty, yet there is a distinction between them. "This unity in multeity I have elsewhere stated as the principle of beauty. It is equally the source of pleasure in variety, and in fact a higher term including both. What is the seclusive or distinguishing term between them?" The answer is "strife," which is in beauty, and which identifies it with life. "To the idea of life victory or strife is necessary; as virtue consists not simply in the absence of vices, but in the overcoming of them. So it is in beauty. The sight of what is subordinated and conquered heightens the strength and the pleasure." [42]

This conclusion is introduced by a famous and difficult passage which associates yet distinguishes between art and nature:

> Remember that there is a difference between form as proceeding, and shape as superinduced; —the latter is either the death or the imprisonment of the thing;—the former is its self-witnessing and self-affected sphere of agency. Art would or should be the abridgment of nature. Now the fulness of nature is without character, as water is purest when without taste, smell, or color; but this is the highest, the apex only,—it is not the whole. The object of art is to give the whole *ad hominem;* hence each step of nature hath its ideal, and hence the possibility of a climax up to the perfect form of a harmonized chaos.[43]

Unraveled and compared with its context in the "Aesthetical Essays," this highly condensed utterance appears as a compendium of Coleridge's entire argument, and of his characteristic movement of thought. "Form as proceeding" and "shape as superinduced" are taken for purposes of definition as different in kind: contraries, therefore, rather than opposites, and irreconcilable. If "shape" is advanced as an adequate principle of beauty it must be rejected. The argument is different, however, if shape is taken as not different in kind but only in degree: a part, an element of "form as proceeding." After all, shape exists in art, and must be reckoned with; its alternative would be shapelessness, as the alternative to regular form would be irregular form, a contradiction in terms. By adding the ideas of life and free will we raise and transform the lifeless shape to the vital form. And the idea of strife enters also with life and free will in the evolutionary struggle up the steps of nature toward the ideal climax.

Art, it was previously maintained, deals not with all nature but with the beautiful in nature, an essence or *natura naturans,* arising from the union of nature and the mind. The "fulness of nature" is too large for the mind to grasp; it "is without character, as water is purest when without taste, smell, or color." [44] It is, in fact, impossible of human realization, though one infers that it is realized by God as his art and creation.

> In this sense nature itself is to a religious observer the art of God; and for the same cause art itself might be defined as of a middle quality between a thought and a thing, or . . . the union and reconciliation of that which is nature with that which is exclusively human. It is the figured language of thought, and is distinguished from nature by the unity of all the parts in one thought or idea. Hence nature itself would give us the impression of a work of art, if we could see the thought which is present at once in the whole and every part.[45]

So, we may recall, "man's mind is the very focus of all

the rays of intellect which are scattered throughout the images of nature."[46] Man can imitate and realize nature only in its parts, or more properly in its orderly steps; but each of these may be microcosm or symbol, idealized by the agency of the universal in the particular or individual (unity in multeity). In this manner art can "give the whole *ad hominem*," can "individuate." Art's function as the abridgment of nature may perhaps be further clarified by an earlier illustration of beauty or symbol as realization. Individual qualities, it was said, are not in themselves beautiful, but conduce to beauty, because they may ideally realize the form without distracting from the idea. "An illustrative hint may be taken from a pure crystal, as compared with an opaque, semi-opaque or clouded mass, on the one hand, and with a perfectly transparent body, such as the air, on the other. The crystal is lost in the light, which yet it contains, embodies, and gives a shape to; but which passes shapeless through the air, and, in the ruder body, is either quenched or dissipated."[47] The translucent crystal would stand for the artistic abridgment of nature, the transparent mass for its fullness, and the opaque mass for the lifeless and idealess *natura naturata*.

# 4

## *Coleridge on Organic Unity: Poetry*

LIFE AND THE BEAUTIFUL, as has been noticed, are identical in their most general definitions, and they are reconciled into identity in their highest (humanly speaking) degrees, as the perfect relationship between the part and the whole. But beauty is of course an abstraction from life and nature, not life and nature themselves. Art imitates not nature but the beautiful in nature, so far as man can grasp it, for "the fulness of nature" is the art only of God. Since it is an abstraction from or an aspect of life, beauty can be differentiated by its limitations. Its immediate end is not truth, but pleasure, and as it has no external reference or interest [1] it is distinguished from the higher good as well as from the lower, agreeable in being without the element of volition. For the "GOOD consists in the congruity of a thing with the laws of the reason and the nature of the will, and in its fitness to determine the latter to actualize the former; and it is always discursive," whereas the "Beautiful arises from the perceived harmony of an object, whether sight or sound, with the inborn and constitutive rules of the judgement and imagination: and it is always intuitive." [2] Life, like the good, is purposive; it is discursive, like the good, in being an evolution toward the end of a higher consciousness, whereas beauty, the end of which is in itself, is thus immediate and nonpurposive. As we have seen, beauty in its higher degrees contains the idea of strife. It imitates the purposiveness of life by endeavoring to conquer all obstacles to its ideal manifestation; but this is a mere simulacrum of purpose, or purpose seen exclusively as a beauty of relationship, for its end remains itself and no other thing. Thus the symbol that is the manifestation of beauty is the ideal or highest degree of actual life as the consummate reconciliation of subject and object, spirit and matter, the mind and nature, but as an aesthetic object it is self-contained and without the evolutionary purpose the idea of life involves. The degrees of life as symbolized in art are self-sufficient, and imitate but do not pursue the road of evolution; the artistic symbol does not in itself force us up the ladder of life. "Each thing that lives has its moment of self-exposition, and so has each period of each thing, if we remove the disturbing forces of accident. To do this is the business of ideal art." [3] Having distinguished the kind, however, conceive beauty now as a degree or a component of life and the reconciliation is performed, for beauty is a means to life's ultimate end of total self-realization, of consummate self-consciousness, and life in its turn becomes in its highest development beauty. "The object of art is to give the whole *ad hominem;* hence each step of nature hath its ideal, and hence the possibility of a climax up to the perfect form of a harmonized chaos." [4]

As one would expect, Coleridge's theory of poetry closely resembles his theory of beauty. "A poem is that species of composition, which is opposed to works of science, by proposing for its *immediate* object pleasure, not truth; and from all other species (having *this* object in common with it) it is discriminated by proposing to itself such delight from the *whole,* as is compatible with a distinct gratification from each component part." [5] So beauty has "the immediate purpose of pleasure," "herein contradistinguishing poetry ["All the fine arts are different species of poetry" [6]] from science, the immediate object and primary purpose of which is truth and possible utility"; [7] and beauty "is that in which the *many,* still seen as many, becomes one." [8] A poem, like beauty, has no end beyond itself:

> The reader should be carried forward, not merely or chiefly by the mechanical impulse of curiosity, or by a restless desire to arrive at the final solution; but by the pleasureable activity of mind excited by the attractions of the journey itself. Like the motion of a serpent, which the Egyptians made the emblem of intellectual power; or like the path of sound through the air; at every step he pauses and half recedes, and from the retrogressive movement collects the force which again carries him onward. "Praecipitandus est *liber* spiritus," says Petronius Arbiter most happily. The epithet, *liber,* here balances the preceding verb; and it is not easy to conceive more meaning condensed in fewer words.[9]

The concluding allusion to Petronious, with its balance of necessity in "Praecipitandus" with freedom in "liber," strongly suggests "the balance, the perfect reconciliation, effected between these two conflicting principles of the FREE LIFE, and of the confining FORM," [10] which appears in the vital beauty and unity of an actual work of art.

Beauty and poetry are not transcendental, as is the good, which is congruent with the transcendental reason and the moral will, because they deal with objects of the sense.[11] The fine arts occupy a middle or intermediate position which reconciles image and idea: they

> belong to the outward world, for they all operate by the images of sight and sound, and other sensible impressions; and without a delicate tact for these, no man ever was, or could be, either a

> Musician or a poet; nor could he attain to excellence in any one of these Arts; but as certainly he must always be a poor and unsuccessful cultivator of the Arts if he is not impelled first by a mighty, inward power, a feeling, *quod nequeo monstrare, et sentio tantum;* nor can he make great advances in his Art, if, in the course of his progress, the obscure impulse does not gradually become a bright, and clear, and living Idea! [12]

Thus imagination, the mental agent of poetry and the arts, is an intermediary faculty, "at once both active and passive"; [13] it "dissolves, diffuses, dissipates, in order to recreate; or where this process is rendered impossible, yet still at all events it struggles to idealize and to unify"; [14] it "reveals itself in the balance or reconciliation of . . . the idea, with the image"; [15] and taste, by which we apprehend the beautiful, is also an intermediate faculty "which connects the active with the passive powers of our nature, the intellect with the senses; and its appointed function is to elevate the *images* of the latter, while it realizes the *ideas* of the former." [16] Poetry and beauty represent the fundamental reconciliation of object and subject, the idealism that is "only so far idealism, as it is at the same time, and on that very account, the truest and most binding realism." [17] They therefore embody the fullest, the most highly organized, and in fact the most valuable consciousness or mental activity, as this activity exists without an interest or ulterior purpose, an object of aesthetic contemplation.

Coleridge's distinction between the primary and the secondary imagination has disturbed some critics, who have been distracted by its abruptness and its grandiloquence:

> The primary IMAGINATION I hold to be the living Power and prime Agent of all human Perception, and as a repetition in the finite mind of the eternal act of creation in the infinite I AM.

> The secondary Imagination I consid
> of the former, co-existing with the co
> yet still as identical with the primary in th
> of its agency, and differing only in *degree,* and i
> the *mode* of its operation. It dissolves, diffuses, dissipates, in order to recreate; or where this process is rendered impossible, yet still at all events it struggles to idealize and to unify. It is essentially *vital,* even as all objects (as objects) are essentially fixed and dead.[18]

Despite much disagreement, however, the "orthodox" interpretation by John Shawcross seems unmistakably correct. "The primary imagination is the organ of common perception, the faculty by which we have experience of an actual world of phenomena. The secondary imagination is the same power in a heightened degree, which enables its possessor to see the world of our common experience in its real significance. And the creations of art are the embodiment of this vision." [19]

One dissenter, a fine critic of Coleridge, has recently argued persuasively that the secondary imagination is not superior to the impressively described primary, and concludes that the distinction in any event is "neither clear nor particularly helpful; indeed, isolated concentration has perhaps distracted attention from other remarks which are potentially more fruitful." [20] If it is a question of "isolated concentration" one must concur, but a firm foundation has been laid in earlier chapters of the *Biographia.* The primary imagination is imagination as Coleridge uses the term psychologically, in relation to other mental faculties. "In philosophical language, we must denominate this intermediate faculty in all its degrees and determinations, the IMAGINATION. But in common language, and especially on the subject of poetry, we appropriate the name to a superior degree of the faculty, joined to a superior voluntary controul over it." [21] The primary imagination is generic, the secondary a higher degree of it. We have seen the same procedure in the *Theory of Life* and the "Asthetical Essays," in the development from a generic definition of life prefigured in the inorganic crystal and culminating at its peak in man; and in beauty on the one hand abstracted in the triangle and on the other fully embodied in the work of art.

The primary imagination is the foundation, the basic conception; the secondary is the heightened and specialized imagination of art, which requires the aid of "conscious will" to realize itself in the artistic product. In the words of Shawcross, the primary is "the faculty by which we have experience of an actual world of phenomena." That is, only through the imagination, the copula between the active and the (relatively) passive powers of the mind, between idea and image, subject and object, can we perceive the outer world as reality. This is the idealism that is the only binding realism, the true common sense. "It is the table itself which the man of common sense believes himself to see, not the phantom of a table, from which he may argumentatively deduce the reality of a table, which he does not see." The true and original realism "believes and requires neither more nor less, than the object which it beholds or presents to itself, is the real and very object. In this sense . . . we are all collectively born idealists, and therefore and only therefore are we at the same time realists." [22]

Coleridge's lofty phrases may seem incompatible with Shawcross's "common perception" and "common experience." But imagination ennobles perception rather than becomes degraded by it. Our consciousness of the world, Coleridge is saying, is a continuous creative act. In his psychology the term "passive" is merely relative. We make the world, not passively receive it, and thus repeat "in the finite mind . . . the eternal act of creation in the infinite I AM," the highest consciousness, the consummate reconciliation of subject and object.

The distinction presents a further problem, implicit in Shawcross's phrase, "actual world of phenomena." The primary imagination is called "the living Power . . . of all human Perception," whereas it is specified of the secondary that "it is essentially *vital,* even as all objects (*as* objects) are essentially fixed and dead." Despite the fact that it is a living power, does the primary imagination see objects *as* objects, as Shawcross apparently suggests, and therefore dead? A simple explanation of Coleridge's emphasis upon the vital quality of the secondary imagination would point to the paragraph on fancy which immediately follows, beginning "FANCY, on the contrary, has no other counters to play with, but fixities and definites." Thus the contradistinction would apply only to it, and not to the preceding statement on the primary imagination. Nevertheless a real issue arises.

M. H. Abrams interprets the "inanimate cold world allowed / To the poor loveless ever-anxious crowd" in Coleridge's "Dejection: An Ode" as his world of primary imagination.[23] But how can a living power be associated with the dead inanimate? It would seem rather to be the world of understanding, an abstraction from the primary imagination, which, not including the conceptions of will and self-consciousness, is merely the datum for the understanding or the secondary imagination. One cannot remain satisfied with it, but must put it to use. Thus in Wordsworth's "Ode: Intimations of Immortality" the glory and the freshness of the child's perceptions are furnished (we may figuratively say) by the primary imagination, which is lost because never firmly possessed; it sees, but does not see what it sees. It fades into the light of common day, and Wordsworth's more passivist psychology provides no secondary imagination to take its place. Only the sense of continuity, a gift, it may be, of imagination, saves the day for him; whereas Coleridge's fuller theory of imagination more fully reconciles immediate consciousness with the self-consciousness that uses it.

As with the primary and the secondary imagination, Coleridge's distinction between the poem and poetry has caused trouble.

> The writings of PLATO, and Bishop TAYLOR, and the "Theoria Sacra" of BURNET, furnish undeniable proofs that poetry of the highest kind may exist without metre, and even without the contradistinguishing objects of a poem. The first chapter of Isaiah (indeed a very large portion of the whole book) is poetry in the most emphatic sense; yet it would be not less irrational than strange to assert, that pleasure, and not truth, was the immediate object of the prophet. In short, whatever *specific* import we attach to the word, poetry, there will be found involved in it, as a necessary consequence, that a poem of any length neither can be or ought to be, all poetry.[24]

Here is an apparent *non sequitur.*[25] We expect the argument to go on justifying the existence of poetry outside the formal poem, but the topic suddenly shifts. One explanation may be found in the context. Coleridge is placing less weight upon the seemingly crucial sentence that begins, "In short," than we incline to do. He is as it were looking over its shoulder toward further observations on the poem: "Yet if an harmonious whole is to be produced, the remaining parts must be preserved *in keeping* with the poetry; and this can be no otherwise effected than by such a studied selection and artificial arrangement, as will partake of *one,* though not a peculiar property of poetry. And this again can be no other than the property of exciting a more continuous and equal attention than the language of prose aims at, whether colloquial or written." The distinction between one property, meter, and a peculiar property of poetry, reveals the connection. The poem, with its attribute of meter, is the appropriate form or embodiment of poetry, the spirit or essence embodied. "Poetry of the highest kind" can indeed be written in prose, but only as an exception; the medium is not perfectly suited to it. The peculiar property of poetry, described "in ideal perfection," is its power of reconciling oppositions by bringing the whole soul of man into activity.[26] The metered poem in its faculty of exciting continuous attention is the most suitable medium for the display and for the reconciliation of these oppositions; it offers "such delight from the *whole,* as is compatible with a distinct gratification from each component part." Variety is impossible without unity. "If in the midst of the variety there be not some fixed object for the attention, the unceasing succession of the variety will prevent the mind from observing the difference of the individual objects; and the only thing remaining will be the succession, which will then produce precisely the same effect as sameness."[27] This unity meter provides, as a fixed object for the attention.

Let us return to the surprising statement that a poem of any length neither can nor ought to be all poetry. It is explicable as an instance of Coleridge's consistent theory of a totality or complex whole which, as we have more than once seen, invariably contains in its relationships the principles of degree, gradation, and subordination. In a totality pure homogeneity is impossible, as a negation of the basic ideas of order and structure. A uniform intensity would be not harmony but monotony. We prize Coleridge's dictum as the realistic, honest observation of a practiced reader, which throws a sudden light upon our own experience. Yet there is a larger relevance in it, for ideal perfection (poetry is described "in ideal perfection") is by definition impossible in actual poems. The conception of "the highest degree" would be a contradiction in terms if it were continuously maintained. Poetry and the poem are in their peculiar properties or fundamental definitions identical, as ideal reconciliations of opposites, but it would be too much to hope that essence and medium should always correspond ideally.

Here the reasoning is the same as the distinction between the ideal and the actual in the symbol. In speculating upon the manner in which such qualities as smoothness and richness entered into the beautiful, Coleridge interpreted them as negative rather than positive agents, and thus in a sense as imperfections. They were necessary, however, for realization. "Something there must be to realize the form, something in and by which the *forma informans* reveals itself: and these, less than any that could be substituted, and in the least possible degree, distract the attention, in the least possible degree obscure the idea of which they . . . are the symbol." [28] The illustration contains three parts: a perfectly transparent body, a translucent crystal, and an opaque or clouded mass. The distinction implies different senses of "ideal perfection." The transparent body is the ideal essence but not the ideal form, which is the translucent crystal, the symbol. But the symbol, the finest conceivable actual form, and thus ideal in a shifted sense, is characterized by imperfections, hindrances to the light yet by which alone the light can be realized. So a poem may be the ideal form but not the ideal itself, which is poetry, just as organization is the highest manifestation of life but not life itself. The parallel between the idea-symbol and the poetry-poem relationship is evident in the quotation with which the account of poetry concludes, from Sir John Davies:

> "Doubtless this could not be, but that she turns
> Bodies to spirit by sublimation strange,
> As fire converts to fire the things it burns,
> As we our food into our nature change. . . ."

This describes a literally ideal symbolization, a complete dissolution of matter into spirit—which is literally inconceivable, like the completely transparent body.

Poetry and the poem stand to each other in the same relationship as subject and object, as life and organization, or beauty and the symbol, and they achieve reconciliation in their basic definitions, or peculiar properties. In dealing, however, with the reconciliation of opposites, one must reckon with what Coleridge called in his law of bicentrality "the two directions of the contemplative act." That is, one's emphasis will be determined by the direction of the approach; one may begin at either end or with either opposite, and go on with it until as a whole in itself it includes the other. If you begin with the poem you conclude by reconciling poetry with it; if you commence with poetry you eventually include in it its objectification in the poem. The famous account of poetry is subjective, and manages without confusion to be an account of the poet, poetic genius, and poetic secondary imagination through their common subjectivity as creative agents.[29] It nevertheless reaches out to include the object, the manifestation, the structure, the poem, as organic unity, as reconciliation, and as harmonious order composed of regular degrees.

> What is poetry? is so nearly the same question with, what is a poet? that the answer to the one is involved in the solution of the other. [Note that relative to the poet his poetry is objective.] For it is a distinction resulting from the poetic genius itself, which sustains and modifies the images, thoughts, and emotions of the poet's own mind.
>
> The poet, described in *ideal* perfection, brings the whole soul of man into activity, with the subordination of its faculties to each other, according to their relative rank and dignity. He diffuses a tone and spirit of unity, that blends, and (as it were) fuses, each into each, by that synthetic and

magical power, to which we have exclusively appropriated the name of imagination. This power, first put into action by the will and understanding, and retained under their irremissive, though gentle and unnoticed, controul (*laxis effertur habenis*) reveals itself in the balance or reconciliation of opposite or discordant qualities: of sameness, with difference; of the general, with the concrete; the idea, with the image; the individual, with the representative; the sense of novelty and freshness, with old and familiar objects; a more than usual state of emotion, with more than usual order; judgement ever awake and steady self-possession, with enthusiasm and feeling profound or vehement; and while it blends and harmonizes the natural and the artificial, still subordinates art to nature; the manner to the matter; and our admiration of the poet to our sympathy with the poetry.[30]

This passage is a compendium of Coleridge's poetic theory, which is essentially one with his theories of life and of beauty. Because this is so, because the passage has been often referred to in earlier pages, and because it is difficult to expound without merely repeating it, my commentary will confine itself to listing the salient points and adding supplementary remarks for clarification:

1) The definition emphasizes activity and wholeness ("brings the whole soul of man into activity").

2) At the same time this activity and this wholeness are manifested in an orderly system of relationships of degree ("the subordination of its faculties each to each, according to their relative worth and dignity").

3) This system is a very comprehensive reconciliation of opposites, couched in both psychological and critical terms. These terms are roughly divided into subjective and objective, synthetic and analytical.

4) As point 2 would suggest, and as is always true

in Coleridge, reconciliation is managed by subordination and assimilation or inclusion, so that one term of the opposition predominates. Thus the ideas of unity, life, and organic unity or nature are dominant here. Art is subordinated to nature; "the manner to the matter; and our admiration of the poet to our sympathy with the poetry."

5) The addition of "discordant" in "balance or reconciliation of opposite or discordant qualities" is not a matter of major importance, but it does indicate an adaptation of the reconciliation of opposites to the needs of poetry and art, since "discordant" is the opposite of "harmonious," and we recall that beauty is a harmony. Poetry is not illogical, but it is not bounded by logic; and whereas logic is discursive the effect of harmony is intuitive and immediate, as would also be the effect of discord.

6) In its reconciliation of the mind as organic unity and the mind as a composition of faculties, and in its subsequent elaboration of oppositions, the passage expresses the characteristic part-whole relationship of the definitions of beauty, of life, and of the poem.[31]

7) Correspondingly, this climactic elaboration implies the element of strife, the struggle to unify, which Coleridge associates with the beautiful, and with the secondary imagination as he earlier defines it ("yet still at all events it struggles to idealize and to unify").

It might be objected that this culminating passage of Coleridge's most celebrated chapter fails to distinguish the organic unity of poetry from the organic unity of reality itself. A parallel definition, perhaps because it is less concerned with the distinction between poetry and the poem, is more explicit: ". . . the proper and immediate object of poetry is the communication of immediate pleasure." The distinction is continued by the observation that poetry is discriminated from any form of science by the preponderance of "those powers of mind, which are spontaneous rather than voluntary, and in which the effort required bears no proportion to the activity enjoyed." This is rather an addition to the previous definition than a contradiction of it. Imagination, indeed, was to be put in action by the will and the understanding, and retained under their control; but this control is gentle and unnoticed (*laxis effertur habenis*), and the effort and the strife themselves are pleasurable. The case may be stated thus: poetry is an imitation of reality, not the reality itself toward which will and understanding are properly directed. These in relation to the poetic imagination are *special.* They are discursive, and their goal as always is realization; what they now aim at realizing, however, is poetry itself, and not their objects in an outer world.

To enlarge a little, the supplementary definition is somewhat more explicit in its statement of the "peculiar property" of poetry, and of the relations between poetry and truth, in which it is comparable to the exposition of "the poetry of nature" at the opening of chapter xiv, and to the account of the "specific symptoms of poetic power" in chapter xv of the *Biographia.* Poetry is distinguished by

> that pleasurable emotion, that peculiar state and degree of excitement, which arises in the poet himself in the act of composition;—and in order to understand this we must combine a more than ordinary sympathy with the objects, emotions, or incidents contemplated by the poet, consequent on a more than common sensibility, with a more than ordinary activity of the mind in respect of the fancy and the imagination. Hence is produced a more vivid reflection of the truths of nature and of the human heart, united with a constant activity modifying and correcting these truths by that sort of pleasurable emotion, which the exertion of all our faculties gives in a certain degree; but which can only be felt in perfection under the full play of those powers of mind, which are spon-

> taneous rather than voluntary, and in which the effort required bears no proportion to the activity enjoyed. This is the state which permits the production of a highly pleasurable whole, of which each part shall also communicate for itself a distinct and conscious pleasure.[32]

The passage is a characteristic movement in Coleridge's thinking. The idea of "pleasurable emotion," as it were the original unity, is dissolved to a duality of object and subject, the "more than ordinary sympathy with the objects, emotions, or incidents," and the "more than ordinary activity of the mind in respect of the fancy and the imagination"; and is resolved again in "the state which permits the production of a highly pleasurable whole." Emotion itself might be considered the unifying agent, a theme that runs throughout. The objective element is emotional as well as the subjective, for it is "a more than ordinary sympathy" with objects. It is well to notice, however, that the emotion is an affair of poetry, and not of life, being such as "arises in the poet himself *in the act of composition*" (italics mine). As in the *Biographia* definition, poetry does not get itself written without the aid of the conscious will and understanding. So, too, the pleasure attached to the poetic emotion or excitement is not merely a "sympathy with the objects, emotions, or incidents contemplated by the poet," but is also a pleasure of the mind in the exhibition of its powers for their own sake, as is hinted in the phrase "full play." It is a pleasure peculiar to poetry, as poetic emotion is peculiar.

Since Coleridge with other romantics has often been charged with confusing art with life, some further display of his position may be forgivable as evidence to the contrary. Thus in chapter xv of the *Biographia Literaria* he makes "a choice of subjects very remote from the private interests and circumstances of the writer himself" a mark of poetic genius. In his *Venus and Adonis* Shakespeare places "the whole before our view; himself meanwhile unparticipating in the passions, and actuated only by that pleasurable excitement, which had resulted from the energetic fervor of his own spirit in so vividly exhibiting, what it had so accurately and profoundly contemplated." Despite its subject matter *Venus and Adonis* is morally unobjectionable, "above all from the alienation, and . . . the utter *aloofness* of the poet's own feelings, from those of which he is at once the painter and the analyst." The same chapter glances at the unity of spontaneous and voluntary in the dictum that poetry "is the blossom and the fragrancy of all human knowledge, human thoughts, human passions, emotions, language"—not, it will be noticed, the roots or the trunk of these.[33]

Meter, the distinctive element of the formal poem, originates in a state of excitement, but an excitement peculiar to poetry, and compatible with volition. Coleridge argues

> first from the *origin* of metre. This I would trace to the balance in the mind effected by that spontaneous effort which strives to hold in check the workings of passion. It might be easily explained likewise in what manner the salutary antagonism is assisted by the very state, which it counteracts; and how this balance of antagonists became organized into *metre* (in the usual acceptation of that term) by a supervening act of the will and judgement, consciously and for the foreseen purpose of pleasure. Assuming these principles, as the data of our argument, we deduce from them two legitimate conditions, which the critic is entitled to expect in every metrical work. First, that, as the *elements* of metre owe their existence to a state of increased excitement, so the metre itself should be accompanied by the natural language of excitement. Secondly, that as these elements are formed into metre *artificially*, by a *voluntary*

> act, with the design and for the purpose of blending *delight* with emotion, so the traces of present volition should throughout the metrical language be proportionately discernible. Now these two conditions must be reconciled and co-present. There must be not only a partnership, but a union; an interpenetration of passion and of will, of *spontaneous* impulse and of *voluntary* purpose.[34]

So likewise it is asserted on the subject of poetic language that

> the very *act* of poetic composition *itself* is, and is *allowed* to imply and to produce, an unusual state of excitement, which of course justifies and demands a correspondent difference of language, as truly, though not perhaps in as marked a degree, as the excitement of love, fear, rage, or jealousy. The vividness of the descriptions or declamations in DONNE or DRYDEN is as much and as often derived from the force and fervor of the describer, as from the reflections, forms or incidents, which constitute their subject and materials. The wheels take fire from the mere rapidity of their motion.[35]

The excitement, though similar to "the excitement of love, fear, rage, or jealousy," is an emotion peculiar to poetry. And it is one of the gifts of poetic genius to distinguish it and to use it judiciously:

> Through the same process and by the same creative agency will the poet distinguish the degree and kind of the excitement produced by the very act of poetic composition. As intuitively will he know, what difference of style it at once inspires and justifies; what inter-mixture of conscious volition is natural to that state; and in what instances such figures and colors of speech degenerate into mere creatures of an arbitrary purpose, cold technical artifices of ornament or connection.[36]

Poetry is a formal art, and the composition of poetry is a measured and premeditated act.

Concerning the role of spontaneity in the poetic process, M. H. Abrams has interestingly pointed out the necessitarian implications of the organic metaphor of the growing plant, and its possible effects upon Coleridge's theory of organic unity.[37] The spontaneous growth of the plant from its seed is predetermined and inevitable, so that if the figure is identical with the theory there is no room for will, judgment, understanding—in short, for "art" in general. "Nature" usurps the whole domain. There is much point in this observation, as indeed there would also be in applying it to Aristotle's concept of form. Correspondingly it has been noticed, usually with approbation,[38] how Coleridge anticipated Freud and Jung on dreams and the unconscious mind.

The question is one of emphasis. If one believes that Coleridge's criticism originates in and is controlled by the analogy or "archetype" of the growing plant, then spontaneity and nature must rule, or must at least so dominate that the critic's struggle to keep them in order is a battle against impossible odds. On the other hand, argument here has shown a careful balance between the spontaneous and the voluntary, and the cumulative weight of evidence upon Coleridge's reconciliations stands over against the claims of spontaneity alone. Coleridge, as we have seen, places great (I think the greatest) emphasis upon self-consciousness, as in his theory of life, which tends gradually upward from the inorganic to the sentient to the incomplete self-consciousness of man, until it reaches the ultimate full self-consciousness of God, significantly termed the great I AM. Imagination "still subordinates art to nature; the manner to the matter;" but "it blends and harmonizes the natural and the artificial." So in Shakespeare, Coleridge's ideal poet, "the creative power [relatively spontaneous and passive] and the intellectual energy [voluntary and active] wrestle as in a war embrace. Each in its excess of strength seems to threaten the extinction of the other. At length in the DRAMA they were reconciled, and fought each with its shield before the breast of the other." [39] The unconscious "is the genius in the man of genius," [40] but without conscious activity it could not be fittingly embodied.

Dependence on the figure of the growing plant to represent organic structure and relationships might indeed overbalance the critic toward necessity and unconscious process. As we have seen, however, in *Theory of Life* and the "Aesthetical Essays" Coleridge clearly differentiates between the creative process in nature and the creative process in man, whose consciousness is his hallmark. And surely his emphasis is unmistakable in such oft-repeated pronouncements as "Shakespeare's judgment equal to his genius," his repudiation of the merely natural Shakespeare warbling his native wood-notes wild. If, also, it is fair to allow his own poetic practice one might point to his demonstrably elaborate revisions of such poems "about" organic unity as *The Rime of the Ancient Mariner* and "Dejection: An Ode."

Organic unity, as has been noted, involves the reconciliation of the concept of life with the concept of beauty, or, in the simpler terms of the great account of the imagination, of art with nature, the manner with the matter. It presents an ideal life, a translucence which is the fusion of image and idea, matter and spirit, in pure substance. Its reconciliation of artistic purpose with artistic material, or the potential with its realization, might fitly be illustrated in the old notion of the perfect statue that awaits the sculptor's hand in the block of marble—it is there in nature, but must be formed and heightened into art. The organic metaphor, as Coleridge uses it, emphasizes not the unconscious necessity of the growth process but its complexity, appropriate to art and poetry in expressing the literally inconceivable subtlety of its being and its creation, the unity and wholeness of the mind of "the poet in ideal perfection."

For Coleridge, then, poetry "in ideal perfection" is, like life and beauty, an organization or organic unity under special conditions and limitations which this chapter has sought to define. More accurately, poetry is like life, and the poem is in its organic unity like organic nature, in which life is manifested. Because it is an idea, like life, organic unity cannot be logically and discursively demonstrated, but must be grasped by imagination in its role as the handmaid of reason. It may, however, be defined as a reconciliation of opposites, and it can be reconciled with the discursive understanding, though not explained or more than partially described by it. That is, the vital connections that constitute organic unity can be only indirectly and figuratively expressed.

The organic unity of a poem is not a dissolution of parts in a whole, or a whole conceived without parts; for such a conception makes analysis impossible, whereas analysis is an element, although *only* an element, of the critical process. The notion of a part is peculiarly important, as the principle of individuation in life, the one and the many in the beautiful, and the whole and the part in poetry have shown. In the method of organic unity, however, the significant parts of a whole, in this instance a poem, are not fixed and predetermined, but depend upon the poem itself as an individual and unique organism. It is in this regard that Coleridge diverges most clearly from Aristotelian analysis, and we see why he calls Aristotle "the lord of the understanding."

A poem is to be judged according to its harmony, or to its unity, or to its fidelity to its own living principle. But there are degrees of unity according to the complexity that is unified and the intensity necessary to unify. Intensity increases in proportion to the obstacles it overcomes, the magnitude of the problems it solves. Thus one judges by a graduated scale of values, from within a kind of poetry, like the lyric, and by kinds themselves, "according to their relative worth and dignity." The living reality of the individual poem, however, makes exact and rigid classification undesirable. According to one's point of view one might say either that Coleridge utilizes Aristotelian classification as the foundation for his system, or that he transforms it into an organic system by the ideas of life and its corollary vital continuity, so that his ladder of individual rungs becomes instead organic nature. Coleridge uses the older, simpler, more objective terms in his criticism, but raises and transforms them. This procedure has been called eclecticism or compromise,[41] but in intention it is something more than these.

Organicism does not mean an anarchy or chaos of an infinite number of discrete organisms. Neither does it imply in its method a crude dichotomy of organic and inorganic, but rather an orderly system of degrees between the theoretical extremes. On the one hand, as we have seen in connection with the law of bicentrality, the individual organism assimilates what it can and repels what it must for survival. The limitations and the apparent defects of a poem may in actuality constitute its individuality and distinguishing quality. The idea of a completely organic work is the theoretical limit, the highest degree, and not an actuality. The passing of judgment, therefore, is not incompatible with the organic method of criticism.

# 5

## *Wordsworth and Shakespeare: Coleridge's Criticism of Wordsworth's Poetry*

IT HAS OFTEN been maintained that Coleridge's criticism of the poetry of Wordsworth is inconsistent with his usual organicist theory and the method entailed by it. Undoubtedly this criticism, which is most fully set down in the *Biographia Literaria,* is on the face of it such as Addison or Dr. Johnson might have written. It looks decidedly neoclassical, with its judicial attitude and its ledger-book balancing of "beauties and faults," along with its appeal to the authority of Aristotle. Coleridge's criticism of Wordsworth's poetry is, nevertheless, entirely consistent with his general position. This issue is crucial, not merely in its consequences for our estimate of Coleridge, but for critical theory and method in general, and, in particular, for contemporary criticism, which is chiefly organicist. If organicist criticism is to be denied the use of analysis, discrimination, and judgment, as Coleridge employs them upon Wordsworth's poetry, it will be rather spectacularly toothless. The present discussion is concerned with Coleridge's practical criticism of Wordsworth, and not fundamentally with his theoretical differences with him. It is not, however, possible to avoid this latter question entirely.

Basically, Coleridge establishes an ideal Wordsworth, or an idea of Wordsworth, and finds him at fault when he does not measure up to this ideal. Coleridge's Wordsworth is a perfect organic unity, a complete fusion of opposites, alive as drawn from Wordsworth himself and not a mere abstraction of the Poet. It is a reconciliation of subject and object or, figuratively speaking, an imitation rather than a copy, incorporating difference with sameness. That is to say, Coleridge attempts to provide not a Wordsworth of literal actuality, but rather an interpretation in which something of himself is infused. Along with an idea of Wordsworth go an idea of poetry and an idea of criticism. The ideal poetry is characterized by universality, and the ideal criticism is a reconciliation of a deduction from critical principles with an induction or intuitive apprehension of the body of poetry to be criticized.

Wordsworth is the ideal poet, but he needs to be distinguished from Coleridge's other ideal, Shakespeare. Briefly, the difference in Coleridge's treatment of the two comes from a distinction of ideal and actual which is applicable to Wordsworth and not to Shakespeare, in whose work the ideal and the actual are almost identical. Thus it is possible to find fault with Wordsworth for not realizing his potentialities, but one can only expound Shakespeare. In practice Coleridge never compares the two, as they are different in kind; Shakespeare is the great objective poet, whereas Wordsworth is the peer of Milton in the subjective and the lyrical. If the final comparison were made Shakespeare would undoubtedly be found to be the greater, on the one hand as a more perfect reconciliation of ideal potentiality and actual achievement, and on the other as a more complex, intense, and comprehensive organism. The comparison would be unfortunate, however, on any but the highest possible level, and Coleridge avoids it.

Wordsworth is potentially the greatest philosophic poet of all times, a unique combination of thought and sensibility. He is the very type of the genius, the choice example of poetic imagination, endowed with the characteristic excellence of penetrating to the true wonder within the apparent commonplace of reality. He is homogeneous and strongly individual, while at the same time universal in his significance. He is a poet for all ages, but as a poet of nature he is a man of his own age, which prizes nature more than art. Thus the idea of Wordsworth corresponds with Coleridge's characteristic idea of organization, or individuation, which unites the universal and the particular, extension and intension, complexity and unity.

Coleridge intends "a fair and philosophical inquisition into the character of Wordsworth, as a poet . . . and a positive, not a comparative, appreciation of their [his works'] *characteristic* excellencies, deficiencies, and defects." In a fair and philosophical investigation "the critic announces and endeavours to establish the principles, which he holds for the foundation of poetry in general, with the specification of these in their application to the different *classes* of poetry." This is his customary reconciliation of unity with multeity, of genus with species, or of wholeness with partness.[1] The critic should then "proceed to particularize the most striking passages to which he deems them [his canons of criticism] applicable, faithfully noticing the frequent or infrequent recurrence of similar merits or defects, and as faithfully distinguishing what is characteristic from what is accidental, or a mere flagging of the wing." A defect itself may be organic to, as it is characteristic of, the poet. "Then if his premises be rational, his deductions legitimate, and his conclusions justly applied, the reader, and possibly the poet himself, may adopt his judgement in the light of judgement and in the independence of free-agency." Coleridge aims beyond the reader at the fundamental problems of the poet himself. As he elsewhere says, "The ultimate end of criticism is much more to establish the principles of writing, than to furnish *rules* how to pass judgement on what has been written by others; if indeed it were possible that the two could be separated." [2] Criticism has the vital function of establishing principles for the use of the writer, not merely the function of furnishing rules for judgment, a function that, without the foundation of living principles, would in itself be mechanical only.[3]

The principles to be set forth are Coleridge's idea of poetry and his idea of Wordsworth. As to poetry, he adopts

> the principle of Aristotle, that poetry as poetry is essentially *ideal,* that it avoids and excludes all *accident;* that its apparent individualities of rank, character, or occupation must be *representative* of a class; and that the persons of poetry must be clothed with *generic* attributes, with the *common* attributes of the class: not with such as one gifted individual might *possibly* possess, but such as from his situation it is most probable beforehand that he *would* possess.[4]

By itself this passage, with its heavy emphasis upon the general, would not be out of place in Johnson's Preface to Shakespeare. In its reconciliation of general and particular, however, it is Coleridge's and not Johnson's version of Aristotle.[5] The exclusion of the accidental from the canon of poetry is calculated to hit at certain lapses of Wordsworth's which result partly from faulty theory. Many of Wordsworth's characters, such as Michael, "have all the verisimilitude and representative quality, that the purpose of poetry can require. They are persons of a known and abiding class. . . ." In poems like "Harry Gill," "The Idiot Boy," and "The Thorn," however, the qualities of the characters are accidental.[6] Wordsworth has been misled by his dependence upon humble or rustic life to supply universality of interest by itself.

From their earliest friendship Coleridge revered Wordsworth as a great man and a great poet. In 1797 he was writing to Southey that "Wordsworth is a very great man—the only man, to whom *at all times* & in *all modes of excellence* I feel myself inferior."[7] In 1798 he spoke to Joseph Cottle of the "Giant Wordsworth—God love him! even when I speak in the terms of admiration due to his intellect, I fear lest tho[se] terms should keep out of sight the amiableness of his manners—he has written near 1200 lines of a blank verse, superior, I hesitate not to aver, to anything in our language which anyway resembles it."[8] This enthusiastic praise has two points of special significance: one, that among Wordsworth's qualities Coleridge particularly admires his homogeneity, so that he almost hesitates to speak of his intellect for fear of slighting his correspondent amiability; the other, that the verse referred to is the lofty and ambitious "Recluse" fragment, which expresses what Coleridge always considered to be the most characteristic (and ideal) Wordsworth.

More than a year later Coleridge repeated his acknowledgment of Wordsworth's superiority, with an accompanying tribute to his personal kindliness. The letter is to Poole, whom it irritated as a friend and partisan of Coleridge, especially as Wordsworth was trying to persuade him to move away from Poole's vicinity to the north of England: "It is painful to me too to think of not living near him; for he is a *good* and *kind* man, & the only one whom in *all* things I feel my Superior. . . ."[9] In March, 1800, Coleridge was assuring Poole that "neither you, or the Wedgewoods, altho' you far more than any one else, ever entered into the feeling due to a man like Wordsworth—of whom I do not hesitate in saying, that since Milton no man has *mani-*

*fested* himself equal to him."[10] At this Poole protested, to be eagerly answered:

> You charge me with prostration in regard to Wordsworth. Have I affirmed anything miraculous of W.? Is it impossible that a greater poet than any since Milton may appear in our days? . . . What if you should meet in the letters of any then living man, expressions concerning the young Milton *totidem verbis* the same as mine of Wordsworth, would it not convey to you a most delicious sensation? Would it not be an assurance to you that your admiration of the *Paradise Lost* was no superstition, no shadow of flesh and bloodless abstraction, but that the *Man* was even so, that the greatness was incarnate and personal?[11]

Coleridge's imagination has lifted Wordsworth above time and commonplace to his permanent position among English poets, and the greatness of the poet and the greatness of the man are one.[12]

Despite vicissitudes and even estrangement, Coleridge's admiration never wavered.[13] Wordsworth was always the great, the ideal poet of the age. Wordsworth's genius, says Coleridge, first led him to meditate upon imagination, and to distinguish imagination from fancy. "It was the union of deep feeling with profound thought;[14] the fine balance of truth in observing, with the imagination faculty in modifying the objects observed; and above all the original gift of spreading the tone, the *atmosphere,* and with it the depth and height of the ideal world around forms, incidents, and situations, of which, for the common view, custom had bedimmed all the lustre, had dried up the sparkle and the dew drops." It is "the prime merit of genius and its most unequivocal mode of manifestation, so to represent familiar objects as to awaken in the minds of others a kindred feeling concerning them. . . ." This excellence is predominant in Wordsworth's writing and constitutes the character of his mind; [15] and one supposes that Coleridge first discovered it as a quality from his experience of Wordsworth. Thus Wordsworth the poet is an idea and yet himself, an individual. His gift is unique, peculiar, yet at the same time a general attribute of genius. He is an ideal reconciliation of opposing qualities, an organic unity quickened into life by Coleridge's long knowledge of his character as well as of his poetry. In the *Biographia* criticism Coleridge says little or nothing of Wordsworth as a man, in the sense of biographical treatment, but his critique is throughout infused with his sympathetic grasp of Wordsworth's nature and individuality.

Many years before he wrote the *Biographia Literaria,* Coleridge had fused the character and the poetry of Wordsworth in a single idea, in a remarkable letter to William Sharp in 1804.

> . . . he is a happy man, because he is a Philosopher—because he knows the intrinsic value of the Different objects of human Pursuit, and regulates his Wishes in Subordination to that Knowledge—because he feels, and with a practical Faith, the Truth of that which you, more than once, my dear Sir, have with equal good sense & Kindness pressed upon me, that we can do but one thing well, & that therefore we must make a choice—he has made that choice from his early youth, has pursued & is pursuing it—and certainly no small part of his happiness is owing to this Unity of Interest, & that Homogeneity of character which is the natural consequence of it—& which that excellent man, the Poet Sotheby, noticed to me as the characteristic of Wordsworth. Wordsworth is a Poet, a most original Poet—he no more resembles Milton than Milton resembles Shakespere—no more resembles Shakespere than Shakespere resembles Milton—he is himself: and I dare affirm that he will hereafter be admitted as the first &

> greatest philosophical Poet—the only man who has effected a compleat and constant synthesis of Thought & Feeling and combined them with Poetic Forms, with the music of pleasurable passion and with Imagination or the *modifying* Power in that highest sense of the word in which I have ventured to oppose it to Fancy, or the *aggregating* power—in that sense in which it is a dim Analogue of Creation, not all that we can *believe* but all that we can *conceive* of creation. Wordsworth is a Poet, and I feel myself a better Poet, in knowing how to honour *him,* than in all my own poetic Compositions, all I have done or hope to do—and I prophesy immortality to his *Recluse,* as the first & finest philosophical Poem, if only it be (as it undoubtedly will be) a Faithful Transcript of his own most august & innocent Life, of his own habitual Feelings & Modes of seeing and hearing.[16]

Wordsworth, then, is a happy man,[17] who has struggled for and won his happiness by framing proper values and by regulating his will in subordination to these values.[18] From his ability to choose, his "Unity of Interest," derives a homogeneity of character which in turn accounts for his originality and individuality as a poet. "He is himself," and need only remain himself to produce the first and finest philosophical poem the world had ever seen. Wordsworth the poet and Wordsworth the man are one. It is not, of course, that Wordsworth's genius, in its aspect as natural gift, is explained by his moral will and insight, but that his genius depends upon these for the power to manifest itself. The spontaneous and the voluntary must interplay.

As the letter indicates, Coleridge's ideal Wordsworth is a great philosophical poet. This Wordsworth differs from the current notion of him, and even from Wordsworth's own conception of his qualities. "It is high time to announce decisively and aloud, that the *supposed* characteristics of Mr. Wordsworth's poetry, whether admired or reprobated; whether they are simplicity or simpleness; faithful adherence to essential nature, or wilful selections from human nature of its meanest forms and under the least attractive associations; are as little the *real* characteristics of his poetry at large, as of his genius and the constitution of his mind." [19] These qualities, whether favorably or unfavorably interpreted by others, are for Coleridge too negative and passive for *his* Wordsworth, at once the real and the ideal poet.

Although Wordsworth's diction uniformly adheres to genuine, logical English, he has not the modest virtue of the "neutral style," or *lingua communis,* as Chaucer and George Herbert possessed it,[20] and as Bowles, Byron, and Southey may claim it. Indeed, to Coleridge it always remained "a singular and noticeable fact; that a theory which would establish this *lingua communis,* not only as the best, but as the only commendable style, should have proceeded from a poet, whose diction, next to that of Shakespeare and Milton, appears to me of all others the most *individualized* and characteristic." [21] Wordsworth's theory of diction falsifies his true bent and practice. Correspondingly, Wordsworth is not a successful dramatic poet because of his strong individuality: "Even in the other poems, in which he purposes to be most dramatic, there are few in which it does not occasionally burst forth." [22] The true Wordsworth is greater than the general view of him, or even than his own aspirations insofar as they are expressed in his theory of poetry. The natural tendency of his mind, despite occasional misguided experiment, is "to great objects and elevated conceptions." [23] Far from being a poet of the neutral style, he is characteristically a poet of striking individual lines and passages; [24] and rather than excelling chiefly at the faithful portraiture of common life, his potentialities lead him toward the production of the first genuine philosophical poem.[25]

Wordsworth's defects both of theory and of practice are defects of his positive qualities. His faults of theory are truths that have been carried beyond their proper lim[illegible] his faults of practice are virtues inadequately
ed and realized. They arise from imperfect
lge of the craft of poetry, and from imperfect
lge of himself as a poet. Coleridge would not
d of Wordsworth, as he did of Shakespeare,
judgment was equal to his genius. In any event,
, Wordsworth's faults are insignificant in com-
vith his virtues; and, "to appreciate the defects
t mind it is necessary to understand previously
cteristic excellences." [27]

efects in question are five: inconstancy or dis-
of style; matter-of-factness; undue predilec-
the dramatic; feeling disproportionate in
to the subject matter; and "mental bombast,"
its and images too great for the subject. The
racteristic, though only occasional* defect, in-
of style, consists in sudden and unprepared
s from lines or sentences of peculiar felicity
style not only unimpassioned but undistin-
He sinks too often and too abruptly to that
ch I should place in the second division of
dividing it into the three species; *first,* that
eculiar to poetry; *second,* that which is only
prose; and *third,* the neutral or common to
One notices Coleridge's typical triadic and
arrangement, with the copula in "the neutral
ch links the opposing terms. Neutralization, however, is not quite the same as reconciliation, and the neutral style is not highly valued by him.)

This defect in Wordsworth evidently arises from his inadequate theory of poetic diction, which makes him offend against consistency and harmony. There is a breach between his genius, exhibited in "lines or sentences of peculiar felicity," and his mistaken artistic judgment and intention. By failing to grasp the distinction between poetry and prose, he violates the canons of organic unity. Wordsworth's inorganic conception of meter is also involved in Coleridge's charge against him. With steady insistence that the act of poetry presupposes per se a heightened mental activity, Coleridge had previously argued that this mental excitement is the true origin of meter. "First, that as the *elements* of metre owe their existence to a state of increased excitement, so the metre itself should be accompanied by the natural language of excitement. Secondly, that as these elements are formed into metre *artificially,* by a *voluntary* act, with the design and for the purpose of blending *delight* with emotion, so the traces of present *volition* should throughout the metrical language be proportionately discernible." [29] Wordsworth's language of real or common life, then, would possess neither the natural nor the artificial components that are proper to metrical language. One may recall as well that "a poem of any length neither can be, or ought to be, all poetry. Yet if an harmonious whole is to be produced, the remaining parts must be preserved *in keeping* with the poetry." [30]

These two passages have expounded *proportionateness, harmony,* and *keeping.* If we now return to his charge of inconstancy of style, we find Coleridge asserting these standards in the slightly altered form of *gradation,* or in this instance *degradation.* The appropriate language of thought and feeling is discordant with the real language of common life. (This is analogous to the disharmony of Wordsworth's poetry.) "But in the perusal of works of literary *art,* we *prepare* ourselves for such language; and the business of the writer, like that of the painter whose subject requires unusual splendor and prominence, is so to raise the lower and neutral tints, that what in a different style would be the *commanding* colors, are here used as the means of that gentle *degradation* requisite in order to produce the effect of a whole." [31] This analogy with the picturesque propounds the language of excitement as it is heightened by art, poetry as it is embodied in the poem, and blending or the inseparable relationship of continuity as it is modified by regular subordination and degree.[32] The result to be attained is an organic whole, in which feeling and thought, nature and art, the spontaneous and the voluntary, are reconciled.

Wordsworth's second defect of matter-of-factness presents two aspects:

> . . . first, a laborious minuteness and fidelity in the representation of objects, and their positions, as they appeared to the poet himself; secondly, the insertion of accidental circumstances, in order to the full explanation of his living characters, their dispositions and actions; which circumstances might be necessary to establish the probability of a statement in real life, where nothing is taken for granted by the hearer; but appear superfluous in poetry, where the reader is willing to believe for his own sake.[33]

In both instances Wordsworth falls into "accidentality," for with objects as well as with persons he misses the ideal and the universal, rendering them only "as they appeared to the poet himself."

In this fault of matter-of-factness Wordsworth is too passive, too purely objective; he depends upon observation and reproduction in detail, rather than upon meditation and vital organization. As meditation and imaginative creation are his real strengths, he evidently fails of the self-knowledge and judgment to realize them in his art. He misses his true ends: how, for example, should the poet select the language appropriate to the emotions of rage and jealousy?

> Is it obtained by wandering about in search of angry or jealous people in uncultivated society, in

> order to copy their words? Or not far rather by the power of imagination proceeding upon the *all in each* of human nature? By *meditation,* rather than by *observation?* And by the latter in consequence only of the former? As eyes, for which the former has pre-determined their field of vision, and to which, as to *its* organ, it communicates a microscopic power? There is not, I believe, a man now living, who has, from his own inward experience, a clearer intuition, than Mr. Wordsworth himself, that the last mentioned are the true sources of *genial* discrimination.[34]

For Coleridge observation is always necessary, but by itself in abstraction it is mechanical and dead. "Minute accuracy in the painting of local imagery" gives us the thing in parts, not as a whole; it is the product of fancy, not of imagination, which is "*creation* rather than *painting,* or if painting, yet such, and with such co-presence of the whole picture flash'd at once upon the eye, as the sun paints in a camera obscura."[35]

Like Lessing, Coleridge distinguishes between poetry and the visual arts. Poetry should not aim at visual effects as such,[36] for these "a draughtsman could present to the eye with incomparably greater satisfaction by half a dozen strokes of his pencil, or the painter with as many touches of his brush." The distinction is vital in establishing the definitions of imagination and organic unity. Word painting, in the sense in which it is here attacked, is copy rather than imitation. It conveys parts only, in separation from one another; it arouses in the reader "a feeling of labor, not very dissimilar to that, with which he would construct a diagram, line by line, for a long geometrical proposition. It seems to be like taking the pieces of a dissected map out of its box. We first look at one part, and then at another, then join and dove-tail them. . . ." "The poet should paint to the imagination, not to the fancy; and I know no happier case to exemplify the distinction between these two faculties." This illustration of the fancy is a mechanical arrangement of pieces in succession, whereas the passage from *Paradise Lost* which exemplifies imagination describes, significantly, the organic growth of and relationship between a fig tree and its seedlings, its "daughters."[37]

The second defect "respects an apparent minute adherence to *matter-of-fact* in characters and incidents; a *biographical* attention to probability, and an *anxiety* of explanation and retrospect." Coleridge's principal contentions upon this point have already been presented, but his argument is extensive. Wordsworth falls into "accidentality," the consequence of his mistaken theory about humble and rustic life. The reviewers, however, have gone the wrong way about attacking him. "To *their* question, Why did you chuse such a character or a character from such a rank of life? the poet might in my opinion fairly retort: why with the conception of my character did you make wilful choice of mean or ludicrous associations, not furnished by me, but supplied from your own sickly and fastidious feelings?" The key phrase is, "not furnished by me." The habit that Coleridge objects to is still extant, and is in fact a chief offensive weapon of those ironist critics who, unhappily inspired by the earlier works of T. S. Eliot and I. A. Richards, have not scrupled to employ destructive associations not furnished by their subject.

Coleridge praises Wordsworth for the Christian democracy of his sentiments, but he finds them wrongly applied in his poetry. It was Wordsworth's "guiding principle, and main object . . . to attack and subdue that state of association, which leads us to place the chief value on those things in which man DIFFERS from man, and to forget or disregard the high dignities, which belong to HUMAN NATURE, the sense and the feeling, which *may* be, and *ought* to be, found in *all* ranks."[38] Wordsworth's purpose is, then, central and universal in direction, but he has made the mistake of arguing like a moral philosopher, instead of representing like a poet. He has tried to ram the pedlarism of the Pedlar in *The Excursion* down the reader's throat by prosy, uneasy explanation, when there was no poetic need to particularize. Thus he has mistaken the immediate end of poetry, which is not truth but pleasure. In challenging the reader's *belief* he has confused poetry with life, whereas the reader needs to have only "that willing suspension of disbelief for the moment, which constitutes poetic faith."[39] A tactless use of biography, philosophy, or religion is fatal: "That *illusion,* contradistinguished from *delusion,* that *negative* faith, which simply permits the images to work by their own force, without either denial or affirmation of their real existence by the judgement, is rendered impossible by their immediate neighbourhood to words and facts of known and absolute truth."[40]

The third characteristic fault of Wordsworth is "an undue predilection for the dramatic form in certain poems, from which one or other of two evils result. Either the thoughts and diction are different from that of the poet, and then there arises an incongruity of style; or they are the same and indistinguishable, and then it presents a species of ventriloquism, where two are represented as talking, while in truth one man only speaks."[41] At first it would appear that Coleridge is determined to impale the poet upon the horns of a dilemma; Wordsworth is to be damned if he does and damned if he does not. And the dramatic form seems to stand condemned in itself. As we have earlier seen, however, the critic's ideal Wordsworth is a lyric, philosophic, and strongly individual poet who should by all means speak for himself. Consequently in Coleridge's view of him he goes against the grain of his own genius when he ventures on the dramatic. His dramatic poems, unbased on his real gift, are inorganic; they violate the canon that "nothing can permanently please, which does not contain in itself the reason why it is so and not otherwise."[42] Either Wordsworth fails completely in rendering dramatic character, and is thus a mere ventriloquist; or if he should succeed with the character he fails to make the rest of the poem harmonize, and thus falls into incongruity of style. Coleridge, one recalls, has earlier adduced the standards of harmony, proportionateness, and keeping; and to these we may add the kindred *congruity*.

Wordsworth's faults in dramatic form are related to his unfortunate "matter-of-factness," since the two come alike from his conception of diction and character, which focuses upon accidental rather than essential attributes of poetry. His fourth defect is also connected with these, and it also results in accidentality and disproportion, as does the fifth. The former class comprises "such as arise from an intensity of feeling disproportionate to such knowledge and value of the objects described, as can be fairly anticipated of men in general, even of the most cultivated classes; and with which therefore few only, and those few particularly circumstanced, can be supposed to sympathize. In this class, I comprise occasional prolixity, repetition, and an eddying, instead of progression of thought." The fifth and final class of defects consists of "thoughts and images too great for the subject. This is an approximation to what might be called *mental* bombast, as distinguished from verbal: for, as in the latter there is a disproportion of the expression to the thoughts, so in this there is a disproportion of thought to the circumstance and occasion. This, by the bye, is a fault of which none but a man of genius is capable."[43]

Both the fourth and the fifth classes are defects of Wordsworth's virtues, as indeed are the others as well. They are distortions of his true form arising from misuse of his true powers. His disproportionate intensity of feeling results in "prolixity, repetition, and an eddying, instead of progression, of thought," whereas a genuine organism must be dynamic and purposefully growing. In his chapter xiv account of poetry Coleridge had said that "GOOD SENSE is the Body of poetic genius, FANCY its DRAPERY, MOTION its LIFE, and IMAGINATION the SOUL that is everywhere, and in each; and forms all into one graceful and intelligent whole." [44] The charge of "eddying, instead of progression" bears some weight, then; it is neither casual nor trivial. Conversely, it may be remarked that the sentence from chapter xiv has more than once been impugned as mere verbiage, whereas it is both central and responsible. One notes with interest the organic metaphor of a clothed human figure that underlies it, a being endowed with body, life, and soul, and more superficially with drapery to set it off.

Of the attributes thus required in chapter xiv Wordsworth is preëminently endowed with the essential gift of the imagination. We have just seen that his poetry at times lacks movement, and we shall see a little later that Coleridge regards him as deficient in fancy. The fifth defect, disproportion of thought, is chiefly a failure in good sense. If Wordsworth describes the experience of "Daffodils" in such lines as

> They flash upon that inward eye,
> Which is the bliss of solitude,

"in what words," asks Coleridge, "shall we describe the joy of retrospection, when the images and virtuous actions of a whole well-spent life, pass before that conscience which is indeed the *inward* eye: which is indeed *the bliss of solitude?*" [45]

Good sense is solid meaning, sound logic, and judicious discrimination. As the "body" of poetic genius it is clearly necessary to its manifestation. Coleridge makes it very evident upon this point that the understanding is not inimical to the poetic imagination, but is an opposite to be reconciled to it, a base for the imaginative structure, a power that sets imagination in action and retains it under "irremissive, though gentle and unnoticed, controul." Wordsworth's occasional fault of "thoughts and images too great for the subject" is a failure of discrimination which may result in the first defect, inconstancy or disharmony of style, as in "Daffodils," where the too-impressive "bliss of solitude" suddenly sinks, "almost as in a medly," to the final lines,

> And then my heart with pleasure fills,
> And dances with the daffodils.

One might well argue in defense of Wordsworth that *pleasure* as he uses it has a meaning both wide and deep; that, after all, the meanest flower that blows can give thoughts that do often lie too deep for tears; and finally, that his poem wonderfully conveys, in the daffodils' rhythmic dance, the motion and the life which are the essence of romantic apperception.[46] Indeed, Coleridge's choice of poems and passages to illustrate this defect are more than usually debatable. Nevertheless they represent important points or stages of his argument.

Thus he attacks a famous passage of the "Immortality" ode as ungrounded and hyperbolical paradox. The child, "a six years' darling of a pigmy size," is reverently addressed as "Thou best philosopher"; and Coleridge, on his guard as he is throughout his entire critique against the merely primitive and passive—virtue by negation—will not allow the ascription to pass unchallenged. In what sense can the child be thought of as a "mighty prophet," a "seer blest"? Surely in no sense of conscious endowment, and if not in consciousness then only according to a pantheism that would equate him with any other being whatever. "In what sense can the magnificent attributes, above quoted, be appropriated to a *child,* which would not make them equally suitable to a *bee,* or a *dog,* or a *field of corn:* or even to a ship, or to the wind and waves that propel it? The omnipresent Spirit works equally in them, as in the child; and the child is equally unconscious of it as they." [47] In the light of the entire ode this may well be unfair to Wordsworth,[48] but it is an excellent example of Coleridge's steady solicitude for the conscious virtues of logic and discrimination.

On these grounds he attacks "splendid paradoxes in general. If the words are taken in the common sense, they convey an absurdity; and if, in contempt of dictionaries and custom, they are so interpreted as to avoid the absurdity, the meaning dwindles into some bald truism. Thus you must at once understand the works *contrary* to their common import in order to arrive at any *sense;* and *according* to their common import, if you are to receive from them any feeling of *sublimity* or admiration." [49] This is a crucial and in some ways a dismaying statement, far more controversial now than when Coleridge wrote it. We have come to place a high value upon poetic paradox.

Coleridge's entire way of thought is against the likelihood that he means to confine poetry to the logic of the understanding, by which it would be subjected to materialism and to scientific abstraction. An idea in his system transcends logic; the imagination goes beyond it; reality outpaces it. The reconciliation of opposites is itself both a paradox and a way of coping with paradoxes. Here, however, as is his method, Coleridge is thinking of logic in two senses, a generic or abstract and a full or real sense, such as we have seen in his definitions of life and of beauty. Thus the latter term may seem to controvert the former, but can be shown to be in keeping as its vital counterpart. One might speak of a logic of the senses and a logic of the ideal, apparently opposed to each other but reconciled into unity by the imagination in poetry or art. This, I presume, is the meaning of the lesson Coleridge learned from the Reverend Mr. Boyer, that "Poetry, even that of the loftiest and, seemingly, that of the wildest odes, had a logic of its own, as severe as that of science; and more difficult, because more subtle, more complex, and dependent on more, and more fugitive causes. In the truly great poets, he would say, there is a reason assignable, not only for every word, but for the position of every word." [50]

What he attacks, then, is baseless paradox which, elucidated, is either false or empty, just as elsewhere he attacks not personification itself but the false personification that is merely an abstraction with a capital letter.[51] He would render to the understanding what belongs to it, and yield it its rightful but limited place in the sun. Rightly or wrongly he considers Wordsworth's child-philosopher a baseless paradox, which he consequently rejects. His passion for unity, too, refuses to be satisfied with unreconciled oppositions, and therefore declines to countenance the *display* of opposition as an artificial exercise of the fancy. The handling of such problems should be responsible, not a feat of legerdemain for which the performer exacts praise. The poetic imagination "still subordinates art to nature; the manner to the matter; and our admiration of the poet to our sympathy with the poetry." To do otherwise would be for it to deny the right of poetry to deal with reality.

"Mental bombast" is not frequent in Wordsworth's poetry, and Coleridge explains that he comments at length upon this fault only because, as it results in paradox and illogical metaphor, it is easy, and tempting, to copy, whereas Wordsworth's virtues are inimitable, being organic and peculiar to himself. "For without his depth of feeling and his imaginative power his *sense* would want its vital warmth and peculiarity; and without his strong sense, his *mysticism* would become *sickly*—mere fog, and dimness." [52] Thus in Wordsworth object and subject are reconciled; his sense as object is vitalized by subjective feeling and imagination, which in turn require his "strong sense" to realize themselves.

Indeed, all Wordsworth's defects are occasional, mere by-products and distortions of his "(for the most part correspondent) excellences."

First of these excellences is "an austere purity of language both grammatically and logically; in short a perfect appropriateness of the words to the meaning." [53] This appropriateness is "the infallible test of a blameless style; its *untranslatableness* in words of the same language without injury to the meaning." "Untranslatableness," [54] Coleridge's prime requirement for poetic style, corresponds with the inseparable relationships of the parts, in which nothing can be altered, in vital organization. He elaborates in an important statement: "I include in the *meaning* of a word not only its correspondent object, but likewise all the associations of the person who is representing it." [55] Language is the object, but the fullest (or poetic language) includes the subject as well, which is sufficiently contained in it. The dictum has interesting consequences for the interpretation of poetry. From its language it is possible to determine not merely a limited and literal meaning but the full meaning of a poem, for it is all within the poem and not elsewhere. Yet only if a subject can be apprehended will it be possible to apprehend a poem as an organic unity. We need, that is, the idea of a poet in the poem, not literally and biographically but as a unifying mind.

Language that is untranslatable is alive by virtue of its vital connections not only among its parts but also with its originating mind. If words are carelessly and superficially employed they quickly degenerate into mere counters or smooth-worn coins of a debased currency; and the poet, the prime user of words, bears the greatest responsibility for preserving and revitalizing their meanings. Unless meaning is preserved by verbal precision, mental accuracy and finally veracity suffer, for the relation of words to the mind is reciprocal: they are created but in turn create. The poet's function as guardian involves the conscious intellectual qualities of good sense, self-possession, and judgment—in short, the virtues of the understanding, indispensable as the instrument of the more vital powers. "Reason can give the *principle* alone . . . while the application and effects must depend on the judgement . . . the greater part of our success and comfort in life depends on distinguishing the similar from the same, that which is peculiar in each thing from that which it has in common with others. . . ."[56] Just as the full logic of poetry is based upon the limited logic of the understanding, the vitality of language depends upon qualities not of themselves vital, but indispensable nonetheless.

Wordsworth's second characteristic excellence is "a correspondent weight and sanity of the Thoughts and Sentiments, won—not from books, but—from the poet's own meditative observation. They are *fresh* and have the dew upon them." This virtue is "correspondent" to Wordsworth's quality of appropriateness in language, to which it is the counterpart. As a gift from nature and not books it is consonant with genuine imitation rather than with literal imitation or copy, as is also implied by the phrase "meditative observation," which fuses the elements of difference and sameness. It will be remembered that the "two cardinal points of poetry" are "the power of exciting the sympathy of the reader by a faithful adherence to the truth of nature, and the power of giving the interest of novelty by the modifying colors of imagination."[57] The dewy freshness of Wordsworth's thoughts and sentiments represents his genius, his imaginative and creative power. Coleridge had previously noticed in him "the fine balance of truth in observing, with the imaginative faculty in modifying the objects observed; and above all the original gift of spreading the tone, the *atmosphere,* and with it the depth and height of the ideal world around forms, incidents, and situations, of which, for the common view, custom had bedimmed all the lustre, had dried up the sparkle and the dew drops." [58]

In this excellence Wordsworth resembles Samuel Daniel, a poet whom Coleridge often mentions with affectionate praise. It is true that Wordsworth is not always as intelligible as Daniel to the average understanding, but the difference comes only from the greater complexity of his thought. The "Immortality" ode is not easy, but it "was intended only for such readers as had been accustomed to watch the flux and reflux of their inmost nature,[59] to venture at times into the twilight realms of consciousness, and to feel a deep interest in modes of inmost being, to which they know that the attributes of time and space are inapplicable and alien, but which yet can not be conveyed save in symbols of time and space." [60] The passage is worth quoting *in extenso* as a concise expression in general of the romantic poet's central problem and in particular of Coleridge's idea of the poetic imagination, both as it mediates and as it struggles to re-create.[61]

It is plain that these excellences are intimately related to Wordsworth's defects, which are disharmonies, distortions, imbalances. When his imagination flags or when he is misled by false theory his "austere purity" of language appears in the altered form of prosaic "sinking," his "meditative observation" as unenlivened matter-of-factness. In the same fashion his third excellence, "the sinewy strength and originality of single lines and paragraphs," [62] is the appropriate opposite to the defect of inconstancy of style. It is notable as an instance of Coleridge's conception of the relation of part and whole, as it is displayed in such a doctrine as his "law of bicentrality," that he finds no violation of organic unity in a method that considers "single lines and paragraphs" in themselves.

The fourth excellence corresponds to the defect of matter-of-factness, especially in "minute accuracy in the painting of local imagery," which was earlier condemned as painting to the fancy rather than to the imagination.[63] In this version of artistic imitation the element of sameness exceeds the element of difference, but it is preserved as imitation rather than as copy by Wordsworth's vital relation to his subject, which endows it with life as well as literal truth. This excellence consists of

> the perfect truth of nature in his images and descriptions, as taken immediately from nature, and proving a long and genial[64] intimacy with the very spirit which gives the physiognomic expression to all the works of nature. Like a green field reflected in a calm and perfectly transparent lake, the image is distinguished from the reality only by its greater softness and lustre. Like the moisture or the polish on a pebble, genius neither distorts nor false-colours its objects; but on the contrary brings out many a vein and many a tint, which escapes the eye of common observation, thus raising to the rank of gems what had been often kicked away by the hurrying foot of the traveller on the dusty high road of custom.[65]

The similes of the reflected field and the moistened or polished pebble present the image with relatively slight alterations, in keeping with the emphasis upon "the perfect truth of nature," while these alterations nevertheless suffice to express the beauty and the individuality of the apparently common object, as it is Wordsworth's peculiar faculty to do.

The fifth excellence of Wordsworth is "a meditative pathos, a union of deep and subtle thought with sensibility; a sympathy with man as man; the sympathy indeed of a contemplator, rather than a fellow-sufferer or co-mate, (spectator, haud particeps) but of a contemplator, from whose view no difference of rank conceals the sameness of the nature."[66] Of the union of thought with feeling perhaps enough has already been said: it is the fundamental reconciliation of head with heart which characterizes the great poet. The defects of feeling and of thoughts too great for their occasions are alike misapplications of it. Coleridge's attribution to Wordsworth of the "sympathy of a contemplator" is at once a reconciliation and a subtle and just distinction, which perhaps accounts for the ability also imputed to the poet of perceiving the all in each, the sameness of human nature beneath the differences, by virtue of the element of aloofness in his gaze. "The superscription and the image of the creator still remain legible to *him* under the dark lines, with which guilt or calamity had cancelled or cross-barred it." [67] This virtue likewise is the obverse face of a defect, the matter-of-factness and the accidentality that mar Wordsworth's treatment of the Pedlar in *The Excursion*,[68] where the poet tries to promote the doctrine of universal brotherhood by arguing the point discursively like a moral philosopher, insisting unnecessarily on the details of his character's trade in order to prove that a pedlar is "a man like ourselves."

Last and climactically, Wordsworth possesses "the gift of IMAGINATION in the highest and strictest sense of the word." He is not, however, in the same degree a master of the fancy, in the use of which he is, as elsewhere, open to the charge of accidentality, on the one hand from excess of thought or feeling, and on the other from his defect of matter-of-factness, manifesting itself in excessive minuteness of detail. "In the play of *Fancy*, Wordsworth, to my feelings, is not always graceful, and sometimes *recondite*. The likeness is occasionally too strange, or demands too peculiar a point of view, or is such as appears the creature of predetermined research, rather than spontaneous presentation. Indeed his fancy seldom displays itself, as mere and unmodified fancy. But in imaginative power, he stands nearest of all modern writers to Shakespeare and Milton; and yet in a kind perfectly unborrowed and his own."[69]

The gift of imagination is the hallmark of genius, yet the disproportion between Wordsworth's imagination and his fancy is a fault, though a noble one. To Coleridge the lower faculty should always harmonize with and support the higher; a gap between them must signalize some lack in the vital organization. Indeed, to play upon his description of fancy as the "drapery" of poetic genius, one might say that Coleridge finds a certain nakedness in Wordsworth's poetry. He both commences and concludes the *Biographia Literaria* critique of Wordsworth with elaborate organic metaphors of natural growth, in which suggestions of harshness and bareness mingle with images of fertility and power.

Wordsworth's genius, he says, was unmistakable in his first publication, the *Descriptive Sketches:*

> In the form, style, and manner of the whole poem, and in the structure of the particular lines and periods, there is an harshness and acerbity connected and combined with words and images all aglow, which might recall those products of the vegetable world, where gorgeous blossoms rise out of the hard and thorny rind and shell, within which the rich fruit was elaborating. The language was not only peculiar and strong, but at times knotty and contorted, as by its own impatient strength; while the novelty and struggling crowd of images, acting in conjunction with the difficulties of the style, demanded always a greater closeness of attention, than poetry, (at all events, than descriptive poetry) has a right to claim.[70]

In Wordsworth, then, there is "an harshness and acerbity," a "hard and thorny rind and shell." This harshness is closely related to potential power, and doubtless Coleridge uses it as an effective and a dramatic contrast to the "gorgeous blossoms" and the "rich fruit" to accentuate the motion of the young poet's promise. It is also true that he goes on to compare the early faults of genius with a self-eliminating ferment, and with diseases that inoculate against themselves.[71] Yet it must be said that a fault remains a fault if it is not eliminated, and the later criticism indicates that it still exists in Wordsworth's poetry.

Coleridge concludes his critique with a passage from William Bartram's *Travels,*

> as a sort of allegory, or connected simile and metaphor of Wordsworth's intellect and genius.—"The soil is a deep, rich, dark mould, on a deep stratum of tenacious clay; and that on a foundation of rocks, which often break through both strata, lifting their back above the surface. The trees which chiefly grow here are the gigantic black oak; magnolia magnifloria; fraxinus excelsior; platane; and a few stately tulip trees."[72]

The deep, rich soil, one presumes, is Wordsworth's genius; the stratum of tenacious clay, his intellect; and the foundation of rock, which often breaks through to the surface, is his basic nature or character, which sometimes manifests itself inappropriately. The gigantic black oaks ("the Giant Wordsworth") represent the characteristic products which imagination combines from his genius and intellect, and the *few* tulip trees are the issues of his relatively sparse fancy.

In keeping with these metaphors of growth, it must be borne in mind that Coleridge is writing of a still-growing Wordsworth, whose development he desires without foreseeing its precise direction. His ideal Wordsworth he can indeed prognosticate in ideal consummation, but this perfection may be thwarted by the poet's imbalances of genius and judgment, or, to put it otherwise, by his failure to divine his own true nature and destiny. When it is applied to men and not to vegetables the organic metaphor of life must manage to include consciousness and free will, including the freedom to err. Coleridge has great but uncertain hopes. "What Mr. Wordsworth *will produce,* it is not for me to prophecy; but I could pronounce with the liveliest convictions what he is capable of producing. It is the FIRST GENUINE PHILOSOPHIC POEM." [73]

For Coleridge the true Wordsworth was the gigantic figure, the unexampled synthesis of feeling and thought, who might fuse philosophy and poetry into a new poetry unique in human annals. He rejected the poet of simplicity and negative virtue whom most of his admirers saw. We now know what Coleridge was unwilling to say in his public critique, although it appears obliquely in his illustrations of Wordsworth's defects—that he was greatly disappointed in the recently published *Excursion,* which seemed to falsify the hopes he had built years earlier on the foundation of the then unpublished *Prelude.* The earlier poem presented the real Wordsworth, the later a perversion of him. What Coleridge expected of *The Excursion* is set forth in his astounding letter of 1815 to Wordsworth himself; what he had found in *The Prelude* appears in the magnificent eulogy of his 1806 lines "To William Wordsworth."

On April 3, 1815, Coleridge wrote to Lady Beaumont, asking her to return his manuscript poem, "To William Wordsworth"—"those lines of mine to Mr. Wordsworth after his recitation of the poem on the growth of his own spirit [*The Prelude*]." His request led him into a discussion of *The Excursion:*

> . . . comparing it with any of the same or similar *length,* I can truly say that one half the number of its beauties would make all the beauties of all his contemporary poets collectively mount to the balance:—but yet—the fault may be in my own mind—I do not think, I did not feel, it equal to the work on the growth of his own spirit. As proofs meet me in every part of "The Excursion"

> that the poet's genius has not flagged, I have sometimes fancied that, having by the conjoint operation of his own experiences, feelings, and reason, *himself* convinced *himself* of truths, which the generality of persons have either taken for granted from their infancy, or, at least, adopted in early life, he has attached all their own depth and weight to doctrines and words, which come almost as truisms or commonplaces to others.[74]

The fault that Coleridge singles out is an aspect of the occasional accidentality that is Wordsworth's chief defect. A certain noble eccentricity in the poet's own experience has caused him to give disproportionate value to "truisms or commonplaces." This defect is, of course, merely a perversion or misdirection of his great and peculiar strength, his ability to find the uncommon in the familiar. Where he goes wrong in *The Excursion* is, as later argument shows, in being too purely "outward," too abstract and overtly moralistic. He presents the "doctrines and words" by themselves, without communicating that depth and weight from his experience which alone could have given the doctrines value. They have not about them "the tone, the *atmosphere,* and with it the depth and height of the ideal world."

Wordsworth, hearing from Lady Beaumont of Coleridge's criticism, sought an explanation of it, which he received in full in a letter of May 30, 1815. Apropos of his own lines on *The Prelude* Coleridge affirms: "It is for the biographer, not the poet, to give the *accidents of individual* life. Whatever is not representative, generic, may be indeed most poetically expressed, but is not poetry." He tactfully applies the dictum to his own poetry, but he is really reading a lesson to his friend.[75] After an accurate paraphrase of his remarks to Lady Beaumont, he proceeds to *The Prelude,* and the expectations he had based on it:

> In order, therefore, to explain the *disappointment,* I must recall to your mind what my *expectations*

> were: and, as these again were founded on the supposition that (in whatever order it might be published) the poem on the growth of your own mind was as the ground plot and the roots, out of which "The Recluse" was to have sprung up as the tree, as far as [there was] the same sap in both, I expected them, doubtless, to have formed one complete whole; but in matter, form, and product to be different, each not only a distinct but a different work.[76]

Appropriately enough, Coleridge uses an analogy from organic growth for "the poem on the growth of your own mind," out of which "The Recluse" was to have sprung as the tree. As usual he both distinguishes and reconciles part and whole in a system of "bicentrality." The two poems were to form a "complete whole," but each was to be "not only a distinct but a different work."

In his 1814 Preface to *The Excursion* Wordsworth had himself employed a well-known figure for organic unity in comparing his poems to a Gothic cathedral, of which the unpublished *Prelude* was the antechapel and *The Excursion* the body. For Coleridge, however, he had mistaken the true relationship. Coleridge had thought of the first poem, *The Prelude,* as *The Excursion,* and of the second poem growing out of the first as "The Recluse," "anticipated as commencing with you set down and settled in an abiding home, and that with the description of that home you were to begin a *philosophical poem,* the result and fruits of a spirit so framed and so disciplined as had been told in the former."[77]

Coleridge had looked forward, he continues, to "The Recluse" as "the *first* and *only* true philosophical poem in existence." In this connection one naturally thinks of Lucretius' *De Rerum Natura,* but whatever in Lucretius is poetry is not philosophical and whatever is philosophical is not poetry. Wordsworth, however, was so to have reconciled these opposites that the *totality* of a philosophical system would not merely have harmonized with but would also have aided "the unity (beginning, middle, and end) of a poem." Thus, Coleridge says, "whatever the length of the work might be, still it was *determinate* length; of the subjects announced, each would have its own appointed place, and, excluding repetitions, each would relieve and rise in interest above the other."[78] The elements of this plan are organic: a form determined from within and growing from the meaning ("determinate length"); a dynamic, evolutionary upward movement ("rise in interest"); and a reconciliation of the parts to a whole and to one another, while each is a whole in itself insofar as its individuality extends ("each would have its own appointed place"). The parts would be interrelated by contrast, harmony, and gradation ("each would relieve and rise in interest above the other"), and their relationship would constitute an ideal organic unity ("excluding repetitions").

This poem, it must be said, could not have been composed by anyone but Coleridge; and he had written or was to write it in the prose of *The Friend,* the first volume of *Biographia Literaria,* and in his essays on aesthetics.

> I supposed you [he declares to Wordsworth] first to have meditated the faculties of man in the abstract, in their correspondence with his sphere of action,[79] and first in the feeling, touch, and taste, then in the eye, and last in the ear,[80]—to have laid a solid and immovable foundation for the edifice by removing the sandy sophisms of Locke, and the mechanic dogmatists, and demonstrating that the senses were living growths and developments of the mind and spirit, in a much juster as well as higher sense, than the mind can be said to be formed by the senses.[81]

This is a scheme of growth (contrast the "sandy sophisms" of Locke with the "deep, rich mould" of Wordsworth's genius); of the correspondence of the mind to nature, and of spirit to sense, as they are organized in a living hierarchy. Coleridge, in short, is describing the idealism that is yet the only true realism.

Building upon this "solid and immovable foundation," Wordsworth was then to have proceeded to "the human race in the concrete." After incidentally exploding the absurd notion that man has developed "from an ourang-outang state," he was to have affirmed "a Fall in some sense, as a fact, the possibility of which cannot be understood from the nature of the will, but the reality of which is attested by experience and conscience." Fallen man was to have been contemplated "in the different ages of the world, and in the different states—savage, barbarous, civilised, the lonely cot, or borderer's wigwam, the village, the manufacturing town, seaport, city, universities, and, not disguising the sore evils under which the whole creation groans, to point out, however, a manifest scheme of redemption, of reconciliation from this enmity with nature—what are the obstacles, the *Anti-christ* that must be and already is." [82] Coleridge never succeeded in understanding the Fall from his own conviction of it,[83] but did accept it as a fact; and he identifies the orthodox Christian doctrine with the romantic belief that man and nature have fallen from their primal unity.[84] His archetype of meaning and of plot was the movement from sin or a fall to redemption, as in *The Ancient Mariner* [85] and *Christabel;* and his letter to Wordsworth likewise contains "a manifest scheme of redemption" from "the sore evils under which the whole creation groans."

According to the theory of individuation, the highest art produces the intensest unity from the greatest complexity and variety, which is represented in this passage by the different ages, states, and circumstances of man, all brought together by the unifying theme of redemption. Coleridge had projected his own ideal poem, "The Brook," in very similar terms:

> I sought for a subject, that should give equal room and freedom for description, incident, and impassioned reflections on men, nature, and society, yet supply in itself a natural connection to the parts, and unity to the whole. Such a subject I conceived myself to have found in a stream, traced from its source in the hills among the yellow-red moss and conical glass-shaped tufts of bent, to the first break or fall, where its drops become audible, and it begins to form a channel; thence to the peat and turf barn, itself built of the same dark squares as it sheltered; to the sheepfold; to the first cultivated plot of ground; to the lonely cottage and its bleak garden won from the heath; to the hamlet, the villages, the market-town, the manufactories, and the seaport.[86]

The brook is a living organism, which possesses on the one hand a perceptible beginning, a middle, and an end; and on the other a vital continuity and an inseparability of parts. It is a growing thing: it is born and proceeds from its source in the hills, and little by little increases, passing through a variety of scenes at once distinct and imperceptibly blended by the gradual movement of the stream. Such, on a still larger scale, was to have been the growth, the structure, and the movement of Wordsworth's great Coleridgean poem.

Wordsworth was to have concluded by

> a grand didactic swell on the necessary identity of a true philosophy with true religion, agreeing in the results and differing only as the analytic and synthetic process, as discursive from intuitive, the former chiefly useful as perfecting the latter; in short, the necessity of a general revolution in the modes of developing and disciplining the hu-

man mind by the substitution of life and intelligence (considered in its different powers from the plant up to that state in which the difference of degree becomes a new kind (man, self-consciousness), but yet not by essential opposition) for the philosophy of mechanism, which, in everything that is most worthy of the human intellect, strikes *Death,* and cheats itself by mistaking clear images for distinct conceptions where intuitions alone are possible or adequate to the majesty of the Truth. In short, facts elevated into theory—theory into laws—and laws into living and intelligent powers—true idealism necessarily perfecting itself in realism, and realism refining itself into idealism.[87]

This remarkable prospectus, poured out as it were viva voce, is a digest of Coleridge's entire philosophy, a prime example of the "all-in-eachness" of his thought, which, like the individual in his "law of bicentrality," struggles at every point and in all conditions to fulfill itself. In its specification of the theme the passage has the incidental interest of foreshadowing Coleridge's Highgate period. In calling for a new synthesis and reconciliation of philosophy and religion, regarded as oppositions of analysis to synthesis, he is demanding of Wordsworth what he himself had lost hope of accomplishing in poetry, and was henceforth to attempt in the prose of the *Aids to Reflection* and his grand project of the *Logosophia.* The passage is a sustained exposition of his ideas of reconciliation and of growth, as it describes a continuous unbroken development from the lowest to the highest degrees of reality, along with the all-important reconciliation between difference of degree and of kind ("but yet not by essential opposition") by which man, as we have seen in the *Theory of Life,* is enabled to stand at once within and outside organic nature.

*The Excursion,* Coleridge thinks, has not achieved

this great organic unity, which would have subsumed all knowable reality in "the colours, music, imaginative life, and passion of poetry." In *The Prelude* Wordsworth has laid a great foundation:

> . . . that Lay
> More than historic, that prophetic Lay
> Wherein (high theme by thee first sung aright)
> Of the foundations and the building up
> Of a Human Spirit thou hast dared to tell
> What may be told, to the understanding mind
> Revealable; and what within the mind
> By vital breathings secret as the soul
> Of vernal growth, oft quickens in the heart
> Thoughts all too deep for words! [88]

But in *The Excursion* he has reared a different and inferior building; he has cut himself off from the soil and the living roots. The second of these analogies is perhaps the more appropriate, for Coleridge's parting criticism taxes Wordsworth with mistaking the part for the whole, as if to exhibit the tree as a dead and detached object. "Your own words," he says, "will therefore explain my feelings, viz., that your object was not to convey recondite, or refined truths, but to place commonplace truths in an interesting point of view. Now this I suppose to have been in your two volumes of poems, as far as was desirable or possible, without an insight into the whole truth. How can common truths be made permanently interesting but by being *bottomed* on our common nature?" [89] The charge of failure of progression is in itself a serious one, considering the importance Coleridge attached to the property of motion or evolution; and the charge of "partness" is a radical condemnation.[90]

# 6

## *Wordsworth and Shakespeare: Coleridge's Criticism of Shakespeare*

The differences between Coleridge's criticism of Wordsworth and his criticism of Shakespeare have frequently been exaggerated, but there is no doubt that his treatment of Wordsworth is relatively judicial, whereas his treatment of Shakespeare is relatively appreciative and sympathetic.[1] In both, however, he employs the methods of organicism,[2] and the differences in his conclusions are inseparably related to the differences in his premises. Coleridge's *ideas* of the two poets are similar yet divergent. Both are ideal and representative, but Wordsworth is the greatest poet of his age, whereas Shakespeare is the greatest poet of all time. In each is manifested a complex organic unity of opposite qualities and gifts—of intellect and feeling, as both are poet-philosophers,[3] and in general of the active and passive elements of mind. In Shakespeare, however, the idea or ideal and the actuality are identical, whereas in Wordsworth they can be distinguished from each other. Wordsworth is not completely harmonious with himself; his tremendous potentialities are in a double sense not fully realized, since he has not "realized" their true direction. Shakespeare attained the perfect balance between nature and art, genius and judgment,[4] but Wordsworth's judgment and artistic knowledge are not quite equal to his natural endowments. As an instance of Wordsworth's slightly lesser organization one might cite his (in Coleridge's opinion) relative deficiency in fancy, which has been noticed in the previous chapter, compared with the perfect fusion of fancy and imagination which Coleridge credits to Shakespeare.[5]

Coleridge, as we all know, has often been taxed with Bardolatry, along with other romantic critics of Shakespeare. The charge is perhaps best met by first admitting it, then glorying in the imputed crime, as the fruits of it are glorious. The term Bardolatry, however, is a play upon the notion of *idolatry*, whereas it would be better to say that Coleridge worshiped Shakespeare as a god whose being was revealed in his works, and then to modify the statement by specifying that Coleridge's Shakespeare is a reconciliation of the human with the superhuman. Idolatry suggests a false and sacrilegious worship; but Coleridge's attitude toward Shakespeare is deeply grounded, consistent in itself, and harmonious with his hierarchical idea of organization, in which the higher is potential in the lower being, as the plant is potential in the rock or the crystal. To Coleridge, Shakespeare, as genius and supreme human being, points upward through graded hierarchies toward God.

As poet and dramatist Shakespeare, that divine, that "myriad-minded" man, "the one Proteus of the fire and flood," is figuratively a god who has created all things and entered into them without losing his identity, a god who is both within and above his creation.[6] Coleridge preserves, however, the distinction between the figure, which nevertheless signifies an absolute human superiority, and what it stands for. Shakespeare was a man who possessed a human, mortal form, although Coleridge confesses that he finds difficulty in imagining the actual, temporal Shakespeare.[7] There is the distinction, too, between the two creations. Coleridge never forgets that Shakespeare's cosmos is a world of poetic illusion.

As a creator Shakespeare enters into his creation while he is yet above it; thus Coleridge introduces him, as the poet, into his poetry and induces his nature from his poetry, yet preserves him distinct as a mind and center that unifies and presides over its organized product. In the same fashion Coleridge's Shakespeare is both within and above his physical and cultural environment as an Elizabethan Englishman.[8] He was a man, he was born, he passed through the natural cycle of growth, and he died; he inhabited places, he wrote for the theater of his time, he had a relationship to other Elizabethan dramatists, he partook of both the virtues and the vices of his age. Yet the essential Shakespeare is immortal and unique, transcending limitations, inspiriting his temporal body, infusing reality with the ideal. Coleridge has little interest in the literal facts of Shakespeare's biography, and is obviously rather pleased than otherwise that so few facts exist; he much prefers the spiritual biography of internal evidence which derives from his *idea* of Shakespeare,[9] a fusion of subject and object; that is, his own interpretation of the evidence of Shakespeare's plays and poems.

Coleridge proceeded thus even with Wordsworth, a man of his own time, in whose house he had lived, an intimate whom he had loved and with whom he had bitterly quarreled: whom he knew, in fact, as an intensely individual private person amid all the confusing traffic of everyday life. The essential Wordsworth was an idea, a poet who existed in time only to master it and mold it to his will. As we have seen, however, even with Wordsworth conceived exclusively as a poet, Coleridge distinguished between the idea and the literal reality, the potential and the existing achievement, whereas in Shakespeare the idea is consummately realized. The case may be put in slightly different terms. As he says of Plato in the *Biographia Literaria,* Coleridge does not presume to an understanding of Shakespeare's ignorance; his mind is unfathomable to him and to all other men. Of Wordsworth Coleridge believes, on the contrary, that he knows him better than Wordsworth knows himself.

Coleridge implicitly conceives of himself and Wordsworth together as opposites whose union would form the ideal poet. He would be the critical counterpart of Wordsworth's creativity, the conscious supplement of his unconscious, the judgment to his genius. He thinks of Wordsworth's poetry as a growth whose flowering has in a measure been thwarted by improper cultivation and direction, so that the plant has failed to achieve the possibilities innate in its seed. Here one recalls the objections to the organic metaphor for poetic creation: that it involves fatalism or automatism, in that the causes of organic growth are either determined wholly from without, or, alternatively, are self-contained, automatic, and consequently inexplicable to reason and to the moral and aesthetic law. In Coleridge, however, in whose thought organic growth is not merely a metaphor or an analogy but an assimilative process drawn from reality, the process moves from the lower to the higher organism, in which, along with the evolution of humanity, consciousness supervenes, and reflective self-consciousness. The great poet is self-conscious to a high degree. His creative genius lies in his unconscious mind, but it is fittingly realized only by an equal activity of his judgment and will. He is at once the plant and its creator, the organization and its life. This reconciliation represents Coleridge's consistent alternation between unity and duality, the movement in which one becomes two and is resolved while yet it is developed into a more complex whole. So Shakespeare is both within and outside his plays, and establishes a mean between ventriloquism and self-dissolution, projecting himself into all things but never relinquishing his identity.[10] Wordsworth, we recall, is sometimes guilty of a kind of ventriloquism from attempting a dramatic projection that is not his forte; occasionally, as in "The Thorn" and "The Idiot Boy," he falls into the opposite fault of self-dissolution, a kind of "accidentality" which one modern critic has termed the fallacy of imitative form, and which in Coleridge's vocabulary would be condemned as copying rather than imitating reality.[11] That is, the picture is accurate, but in attaining accuracy the painter has sacrificed his own superior intellect and imagination to a lower state of being. Shakespeare is never guilty of this fault. He achieves artistic triumphs in characters analogous to Wordsworth's simple rustics: in the Nurse and in Mistress Quickly, for example, in whom he portrays inconsequence without being inconsequential.[12]

Thus Coleridge's criticism of Shakespeare is basically sympathetic and appreciative. It could hardly be otherwise, for it arises from the firm persuasion that Shakespeare is the greatest genius the world has ever known. In the light of his own experience Coleridge hesitates to attribute defects to Shakespeare, because he has learned that when he has done so in the past he himself has usually been guilty of misunderstanding.[13] The study of Shakespeare is a gradually evolving process of enlightenment, continually revealing new relationships earlier unperceived. Coleridge does see faults in Shakespeare, however, when after due deliberation he can find no justification that fits his idea or hypothesis. He recoils from the scene of the blinding of Gloucester in *Lear*, and he finds the porter scene of *Macbeth* out of keeping with his conception of the play.[14] Indeed, his specific intention in dealing with Shakespeare is to point out merits and defects, not merely to expound.[15] Coleridge's Shakespeare criticism makes his usual subtle and careful distinctions, and differs from his criticism of Wordsworth only in proportion to the difference in his critical objectives.

In his treatment of Shakespeare, Coleridge pursues

his customary method of reconciling unity with multeity. Shakespeare is like organic nature according to the "law of bicentrality," in which every part has a center or principle both within and outside itself, like a system of concentric circles of which the master circle would be the total idea of Shakespeare. Within this all-inclusive unity there would be various lesser unities and systems, each self-contained and yet a part in a graduated structure of subordination and degree which ranges from the lowest to the highest, from the simplest to the most complex. Like the principle of life, Shakespeare is almost infinitely various [16] and yet forever the same. To express this reconciliation, which is abstractly life's attribute of individuation, Coleridge in his Shakespeare criticism recurs continually to the figure of Proteus, "who now flowed, a river; now raged, a fire; now roared, a lion—he assumed all changes, but still in the stream, in the fire, in the beast, it was not only the resemblance, but it was the divinity that appeared in it, and assumed the character." [17]

In defining Shakespeare's poetic character, Coleridge, as is his habit, reconciles kind and degree, and the individual with the universal. Shakespeare is the greatest, the ideal poet, but he is not therefore characterless. He is predominantly objective, whereas Milton and Wordsworth are subjective poets; he is a man of his time, although he almost completely masters it; and his verse is so strongly individual that it is possible to establish the Shakespeare canon from it in passages of disputed authorship. Coleridge's reliance upon internal evidence is excessive, as all have agreed. In employing it he is following the doctrines of organicism, but he transgresses against his own conception of the balance between subject and object in his too-exclusive preference for the evidence of internal relationships. In attempting to establish a chronology of the plays upon a psychological theory of Shakespeare's development he tries to stretch criticism beyond its bounds, for under the circumstances all theoretical inference must supplement fact rather than try to supplant it. His error, however, is at any rate consistent with his method, though he mistakes its application. It is not wholly defensible, but it is preferable to the false chronological organicism of the professional scholar, which deprives the so-called organic growth of head and direction and consequently of life, and makes the history of a poet's development a negative exercise in the avoidance of pitfalls instead of a positive discovery of values.

Coleridge thus conceives of Shakespeare in three different perspectives: as universal genius, as Elizabethan, and as individual. His universality is tempered only by his character of objectivity; and this qualification is necessary, for only God presents the perfect balance of subject and object. As a man of his own age he partakes of its advantages and is affected by its faults, as in his occasional grossness and addiction to the verbal ingenuities of punning and conceits.[18] Correspondingly his plays are universal in complexity and comprehensiveness, but they belong to the class of romantic drama,[19] which in turn contains the subclasses of tragedy, comedy, the history play, and even farce in *The Comedy of Errors.*[20] Coleridge uses the idea of romantic drama in the double sense that has been noted in connection with his reconciliation of opposites; that is, generically it is the opposite of classical drama, but in its superior complexity and intenser unity it is the synthesis and reconciliation itself. *The Tempest* is his grand example of romantic drama, because it is freest from the sensory bonds of time and space and, in its more ideal relationships, presents the perfect triumph of poetic art,[21] but all the plays are romantic in their character of "intermixture" and unified heterogeneity. Within this scheme each play possesses its own idea and individuality, while it likewise has vital connections with other plays.[22] So *Hamlet* and *Macbeth* are polar opposites of inner and external action and of motion, and *King Lear* stands midway between them; and *Romeo and Juliet* is the opposite to *Antony and Cleopatra.*[23] The same pattern appears in Coleridge's treatment of Shakespeare's characters. Each character is at once a symbol of universal human nature, the representative of a class, and an individual. The centrality of Shakespeare's plays is the centrality of the passions [24] portrayed in them, individualized in character in inexhaustibly different combinations.

For Coleridge a Shakespeare play is a romantic drama and an organic unity, a living plant evolved from an idea. Coleridge uses various figures to express this organic unity, or unity of interest: a harmonious natural scene, a portrait, a single plant, a spreading banyan tree with its seedlings springing up about it, a cultivated English garden fusing nature and art, a Gothic cathedral, a splendid sunrise, and a sinuously winding serpent.[25] Perhaps the chief quality of a Shakespeare play, as Coleridge views it, is fluidity of movement.[26] It is an infinitely complex set of evolving relationships, a continuous progressive motion with continual subtle changes of direction. Coleridge's grasp of the living, close-knit, uncoiling and recoiling movement of a developing play is perhaps most like Harley Granville-Barker's among modern critics, despite the difference in their attitudes toward theatrical performance. Coleridge is aware of a perpetual subtle modulation, in preparation,[27] contrast,[28] gradation,[29] fusion of difference and sameness, shift of tempo, and raising and lowering of intensity,[30] resulting in a complex unity-in-variety that synthesizes while permitting the parts of the whole an existence in and for themselves.

This multiple and varied movement is directed. A play begins from a germ or idea [31] which potentially contains the whole. This germ may be predominantly psychological, or moral, or metaphysical, but it is in every important instance a fusion of all three. The famous disability of Hamlet is psychological in its disproportion between perception and introspection, metaphysical in imbalance of subject and object, and moral in its effect upon Hamlet's actions. The germ of a play is a disproportion or disequilibrium in a single character, or between characters, or in a set of circumstances. In *Romeo and Juliet* it is family life itself, with no opposing force to counter it, which sets the old upon the young; [32] in *Othello* the germ lies in Iago, whose intellect and will are unbalanced by passion and morality.[33] In *Troilus and Cressida* the love of Troilus has no counterpart in Cressida's merely accidental passion, which fixes quickly upon another object when the original object is withdrawn.[34] The idea of a play, its intellectual identity, is joined with its feeling, the springlike quality of *Romeo and Juliet,* and its character, precipitation, which suits its characters as does the deliberate movements of *Hamlet.*[35]

All the characters of a Shakespeare play are related to its central idea and to one another, by contrast, balance, likeness, modification, and subordination. Each character has his own being and individuality; as in the law of bicentrality he is subordinate but not enslaved to the purposes of the whole. He has a center in himself which is his life. Coleridge's adherence to this principle of bicentrality, the reconciliation of wholeness with partness,[36] is apparent in his numerous references to "lyric movements," such as Polonius' advice to Laertes, and in his constant interest in meter, which exists expressively but also as an element in itself.[37] Coleridge points out that whenever possible Shakespeare reconciles the expressive function of meter with a self-exhibiting regularity.[38]

T. M. Raysor, the indispensable editor of Coleridge's Shakespearean criticism, has remarked that Coleridge has no interest in structure, and neglects it completely.[39] One might quite as reasonably assert that Coleridge discusses nothing but structure, and that his whole account of the Shakespearean drama is a description of its organic interrelations. The argument would rest, however, upon a misunderstanding about the meaning of *structure* as it is being used. Mr. Raysor is apparently thinking of plot, or external action abstracted from the substance of the play, in some such formulation as A. C. Bradley's adaptation of Aristotle, in which one settles upon focal points like rising and falling action, complication, crisis, retarding point, climax, denouement, and the like. These are useful tools of analysis, but Coleridge is aiming at a more closely woven and vital unity than they could serve to convey. Recent critics have tended to agree with him, even though they customarily come from the direction of Aristotle. More and more one hears of a "unity of action" far broader than the abstract relationships of plot, and distinguishable from Coleridge's unity of interest [40] only in the location of its starting point.

Coleridge's criticism of Shakespeare has been charged, as has nineteenth-century criticism in general, with heresy in its emphasis upon character. The charge would be true only if it could be shown that character is isolated by him from the other elements of a play, as heresy is the disproportionate emphasis upon a single truth. Like the great English Victorian novelists, Coleridge seeks to conceive a full, vital, and multidimensional imitation of life, and to do so he brings art and life as near each other as it is safe to do without confusing the two. He thinks of the drama as an ideal imitation of the permanent elements of human nature under the influence of passion, or, as Wordsworth would say, in a state of excitement. He feels that Shakespeare was relatively regardless of story, the skeleton of arranged events with which he commences, and therefore he feels justified in neglecting the mere canvas of the artist's painting. Even plot, which is closer to Shakespeare's use of his story, is still too abstract for his purposes. But Coleridge does not devote himself exclusively to character as isolated and static;

rather he treats of character in motion and action, dynamically developing in a variety of relationships with other characters, with circumstances, and with external events. Whereas for Aristotle drama is a human action, for Coleridge it is human character in action. As critic and exponent of the romantic drama he is faithful to his subject, as was Aristotle to the plays upon which he based his theory. The peculiar solidity and fullness of Shakespeare's characterizations are of course illusions [41] in Coleridge's own artistic sense, but his characters are no mere inventions of subjectivist critics; they tempt us to take them for real beings. It is undoubtedly artistically wrong and sinful to permit Falstaff to run away with the *Henry IV* plays, but it is a tribute to his power and his vitality that so many have been captivated by him into neglecting the larger whole in which he exists.

Coleridge himself, however, never makes this error. His conception of dramatic character is consonant with his general way of thought: his identification of artistic means with ends, and his perception of totality as the reconciliation of partness and wholeness. Character is a means to the end of dramatic illusion, but at the same time it exists for itself as a condition of its vitality.

Coleridge's celebrated theory of dramatic illusion was doubtless formulated to deal with the problem of Shakespeare and "the three unities." The unities of time, place, and action so dear to the hearts of the French were, he felt, based on a doctrine of literal delusion, mistakenly supposing that the audience is deceived into taking the play as a real happening. Dr. Johnson, on the other hand, in his Preface to his edition of Shakespeare, had maintained that a theatrical audience was never deceived for a moment. The spectator understood that he was viewing a presentation of fictional events, and judged it according to its adherence to sound morality, logical probability, and general human nature. For Coleridge the truth was a reconciliation of these two extreme views: the audience of a play is neither deceived nor wholly undeceived about its reality. It is in a state of *illusion,* a complex attitude in part self-willed, in part created by the skill of the playwright and the actors.

Coleridge discusses the question of dramatic illusion in substantially the same terms in various places at different periods of his thought; his opinions in this regard are at all times self-consistent. An introduction to *The Tempest* for his 1818–19 lecture course is representative. *The Tempest,* he commences, is "a specimen of the romantic drama." At this point he immediately turns aside; not, however, without justification in the nature of the topic. "But whatever play of Shakespeare's we had selected there is one preliminary point to be first settled, as the indispensable condition. . . . This point is contained in the words probable, natural." His conception of *The Tempest* as romantic, with its consequent imputation of improbability, raises a difficulty. That Shakespeare is faithful to nature is unshakable dogma. As applied to drama, then, *natural* and *probable* do not have their ordinary meanings; and thus we enter upon the problem of dramatic illusion.

The drama is an imitation, not a copy of reality—"and that imitation is contradistinguished from copy by this: that a certain quantum of difference is essential to the former, and an indispensable condition and cause of the pleasure we derive from it; while in a copy it is a defect, contravening its name and purpose." Aesthetically speaking, we prefer a still-life to a marble peach, a painting to a waxwork figure. And thus of the drama: certain improbabilities belong to it as an art. Of this, for example, "we need no other proof than the impassive slumber of our sense of probability when we hear an actor announce himself as a Greek, Roman, Venetian, or Persian in good mother English."

There is, however, "a sort of improbability with which we are shocked in dramatic representation no less than in the narrative of real life." (Coleridge does not say so, but we are here confronted with the distinction of accidental and essential improbability or, alternatively, with the difference between the artistic and the inartistic. The derivation is ultimately from the *Poetics,* but with an important difference. Aristotle is willing to excuse a trivial improbability to achieve an artistic end, but he would still prefer the truth of logic and science if it will square with artistic imitation. For Coleridge, on the other hand, a modicum of literal improbability is necessary to imitation, not merely a trivial fault to be generously tolerated. In this respect he is both Platonic and romantic, not Aristotelian. His distinction owes something to the Platonic difference between appearance and reality, and something to the romantic imagination, which glories in its power over literal improbabilities.)

As previously, Coleridge now apparently steps aside, but in reality he is approaching the heart of his argument. Dramatic illusion is analogous to dream, but distinguishable in that dream is the *highest degree* of illusion. We do not take our dreams for realities, for sleep suspends the voluntary and therefore the comparative power. "The fact is that we pass no judgement either way: we simply do not judge them to be unreal. . . . In sleep we pass at once by a sudden collapse into this suspension of will and the comparative power: whereas in an interesting play, read or represented, we are brought up to this point, as far as it is requisite or desirable, gradually, by the art of the poet and the actors; and with the consent and positive aidance of our own will. We *choose* to be deceived." Now comes the suspended definition of essential improbability, the sort "with which we are shocked in dramatic presentation." "Whatever tends to prevent the mind from placing it[self] or from being gradually placed in this state in which the images have a negative reality must be a defect, and consequently anything that must force itself on the auditors' mind as improbable, not because it *is* improbable (for that the whole play is foreknown to be) but because it cannot but *appear* as such." (One recalls the *Poetics* on the superiority of probable impossibilities to improbable possibilities.)

The question of improbability depends, however, "on the degree of excitement in which the mind is supposed to be." Some things are permissible in midplay, others in the opening scene. "Many things would be intolerable in the first scene of a play that would not at all interrupt our enjoyment in the height of the interest. The narrow cockpit may hold

> The vasty fields of France, or we may cram
> Within its wooden O the very casques
> That did affright the air at Agincourt.

And again, on the other hand, many obvious improbabilities will be endured as belonging to the groundwork of the story rather than to the drama, in the first scenes, which would disturb or disentrance us from all illusion in the acme of our excitement, as, for instance, Lear's division of his realm and banishment of Cordelia." Coleridge for the moment leaves us to infer the positive function of such improbabilities as these, without explanation. Shortly afterward, however, we learn their use in the total work. In addition to the dramatic probability negatively achieved by good judgment in the apportionment of improbabilities, all other excellencies of the drama, "as unity of interest, with distinctness and subordination of the characters, appropriateness of style, nay, and the charm of language and sentiment for their own sakes, yet still as far as they tend to increase the inward excitement, are all means to this chief end, that of producing and supporting this willing illusion."

This is a thoroughly contemporary-sounding pronouncement in its heavy emphasis upon organic functionalism, that shibboleth of our critical age. To it, however, is appended a characteristically Coleridgean qualification, which at the same time subtly shifts again to the theme of functionality or, more Coleridgeanly, proportionateness. In a work of art means are not fundamentally distinguishable from ends; to speak more strongly, in such a work the means and the end are identical. Thus, although the "excellencies" mentioned above are means toward the end of dramatic illusion, "they do not therefore cease to be themselves ends, and as such carry their own justification with them as long as they do not contravene or interrupt the illusion. It is not even always or of necessity an objection to them, that they prevent it from rising to as great a height as it might otherwise have obtained; it is enough, if they are compatible with as high a degree as is requisite."

This passage, and what follows, has its difficulties. Having specified illusion as the chief end of drama, Coleridge now seems to be suggesting some other end as more important. "As high a degree as is requisite" hints that illusion itself is merely a means, a fastener of interest and sympathy in the service of a further purpose. In ultimate terms, the possibility cannot be dismissed that Coleridge is suggesting precisely this. Yet he continues with an explanation that restores improbability to its functional role, as a preserver of emphasis and proportion. "If the panorama had been invented in the time of Leo X, Raphael would still have smiled at the regret that the broom-twigs, etc., at the back of his grand pictures were not as probable trees as those in the panorama. Let me venture to affirm that certain obvious, if not palpable, improbabilities may be hazarded in order to keep down a scene, [to keep it] merely instrumental, and to preserve it in its due proportion of interest." The implication is, then, that an illusion equally maintained at all points would be self-defeating: proportionless, featureless, structureless, without the unity upon which illusion itself depends. Dramatic illusion must arise from delicate gradations, subordinations, a subtle symmetry.

For Coleridge dramatic illusion is essentially the same as artistic illusion in general, the counterpart of imitation as the principle of art. There is, however, a distinction to be made; the *degree* of illusion is higher, for example, in the theater than in painting. But first, to follow Coleridge's own order of thought, one should speak of his notion of the stage. (The passages to follow come from two much earlier fragments, which may belong to the lecture course of 1808. They supplement without contradicting the account that has so far been used.) The stage, says Coleridge, is "a combination of several, or of all the fine arts to an harmonious whole having a distinct end of its own, to which the peculiar end of each of the component arts, taken separately, is made subordinate and subservient; that, namely, of imitating reality (objects, actions, or passions) under a *semblance* of reality." Stage illusion is more complete than, for instance, the illusion provided by a landscape painting: "Thus, Claude imitates a landscape at sunset, but only as a *picture;* while a forest-scene is not presented to the audience as a picture, but as a forest." Stage presentations "are to produce a sort of temporary half-faith, which the spectator encourages in himself and supports by a voluntary contribution on his own part, because he knows that it is at all times in his power to see the thing as it really is." Coleridge continues with some subtle distinctions of degrees of illusion. Children can be deceived by stage scenery but never by pictures; yet the "child, if strongly impressed, does not indeed positively think the picture to be the reality; but yet he does not think the contrary." Now, what pictures are to children, stage illusion is to men, "provided they retain any part of the child's sensibility, except that in the latter instance this suspension of the act of comparison, which permits this sort of negative belief, is somewhat more assisted by the will than in that of the child respecting a picture."

As with most of Coleridge's best ideas, it has been strongly hinted of his theory of dramatic illusion that it is no more original than it should be. René Wellek has suggested anticipation by Mendelssohn, and in her *Coleridge, Opium, and Kubla Khan* Elisabeth Schneider finds her subject ungenerously silent about his knowledge of the writings of Erasmus Darwin. This is not the place to discuss the tortured question of Coleridge's "plagiarism," but two summary remarks may be in order. First, the multiplicity of his possible sources is so great as to neutralize the effect of any one in particular. Among Englishmen, Twining, Dryden, Beattie, and Knight, as M. H. Abrams points out in *The Mirror and the Lamp,* had discussed the state of mind of a theatrical audience and the acceptance of improbabilities, and from Kames onward the British empiricists had considered the relations of dream and imagination; and it is needless to speak of Coleridge's acquaintance with German transcendental aesthetics. Add to this Plato and Aristotle, and one comes up with a substantial portion of the intellectual heritage of Western man. The vitality, the subtlety, and the concreteness of Coleridge's treatment of dramatic illusion are self-validating; it is organically alive both in itself and in its close relationship with Coleridge's whole way of thinking. This latter relationship is perhaps beyond the scope of this essay, at least for its own sake. Yet some notion of the place of the theory of illusion in Coleridge's thought is necessary to identify the theory itself, and it may also be expedient to say in advance that the theory is only a basis for the practice of his criticism.

The inception of the idea as a reconciliation of or a mean between the two opposite views of the French neoclassics and Johnson is highly characteristic, for Coleridge's habitual dialectic is a demonstration of relationships between apparent disparates. While carefully maintaining necessary distinctions, he seeks to establish the essential unity of many concepts usually regarded as separate. Thus his criticism evolved in part as a correction of the categories of neoclassical criticism, such as nature-art, or genius-judgment. Imitation itself he treated as a reconciliation of nature and art, and he delighted in explaining that "Shakespeare's judgment was equal to his genius." Truth, Coleridge felt, generally lies in the middle, and falsehood, or at least distortion, in extremes. Furthermore, as he was seldom tired of remarking, extremes meet, as the sensations of touching extremely hot or extremely cold water are identical. The French theory of complete deception of the audience would produce the same result as Johnson's theory of no deception whatever. In either instance a play would have to conform to the criteria of literal, common-sense reality.

As has been earlier suggested, Coleridge's subtle compromise between belief and unbelief in the matter of dramatic illusion is applicable to his theory of imitation in general. We are most familiar with his description of the appropriate attitude toward poetry, the "willing suspension of disbelief for the moment, which constitutes poetic faith." This double negative that makes a positive, complicated by the further issue of "willing," is important at once in maintaining the distinction between art and truth upon which Coleridge steadily insisted—"A poem is that species of composition, which is opposed to works of science, by proposing for its immediate object pleasure, not truth"—and at the same time in leaving open the possibility of truths of the imagination, which complement and explain the phrase "poetic faith." Thus the literally impossible may have poetic or dramatic truth: ". . . the incidents and agents were to be, in part at least, supernatural; and the excellence aimed at was to consist in the interesting of the affections by the dramatic truth of such emotions, as would naturally accompany such situations, supposing them real." We recall the distinction cited earlier in this essay between the literal and the dramatic application of the words "natural" and "probable." This is a necessary differentiation, in the manner of Aristotle. One should not ignore, however, the Platonic hint that the dramatic and poetic truth is the real, the essential, whereas the literal or scientific truth is merely apparent and extraneous.

In two other important particulars Coleridge's theory of dramatic illusion is typical of his general thought. Both manifest his ever-present urge toward synthesis. First, his idea of illusion reconciles means and ends, partness and wholeness. As we have seen, he conceives the stage as a synthesis of the arts for the purpose of illusion, but permits each art to remain an end in itself while serving an end beyond itself, just as, to present a single example, his most celebrated account of the imagination reconciles faculty psychology with a concept of the mind as a single organism. Second, and crucial, his theory of dramatic illusion employs the subject-object distinction that underlies his entire method of thought, and is vital to his aesthetics. This is perhaps a commonplace, but the nature of good subject-object criticism remains much misunderstood.

The chief point to be made about it is that it envisages two coequal realities, each incomplete without the other, and reconcilable as one. It is not simply psychological or purely subjective. If it commences with an effect, it looks for its cause; if it talks of unity of interest, it seeks to penetrate to the source of the interest and the elements and relationships composing the unity. Thus Coleridge's doctrine of illusion supposes the audience, or a spectator, the subject, and a play the object. The immediate purpose of their conjunction is dramatic illusion. Each is of itself incomplete: the play requires the will, to a degree the "good will," of the spectator to fulfill its end; the spectator requires for his experience of illusion a unified object, a complex of elements composed in harmony. Dramatic or other criticism will then be both subjective and objective: psychological and introspective as the critic examines his own state of mind, but also formalist as he appraises the external structure or organization that causes it. It will be an affective criticism, as it talks of the spectator's feelings and emotions, but it will also be a structural criticism in its assumption of an objective equivalent to these feelings.

Coleridge has left us no formally complete interpretations of individual plays by Shakespeare, although his method anticipates and is an important source for the elaborate dialectical "explications" of modern critics. There are of course simple, matter-of-fact explanations for this incompleteness: his physical and psychological state during most of the period of his lectures on Shakespeare; his immediate purpose of effective presentation to lecture audiences; and the consequent limitation of his recorded criticism to letters, notes, marginalia in editions of Shakespeare, more or less accurate reports of his lectures by different hands, and reports and reminiscences of his conversation. More fundamentally, however, it was his conviction that literal completeness of interpretation was death, mere copy rather than creative imitation. He says enough to clear the way, and leaves the rest to his listener or reader, providing sufficient concrete interpretation to verify his hypotheses. He gives disproportionate attention to opening scenes, in keeping, as one critic has interestingly suggested, with the genetic tendency of his thought. It can also be said that his emphasis comes from his consistent care to demonstrate Shakespeare's artistic judgment. The establishment of dramatic and poetic illusion is a vital consideration, and this work must of course be accomplished at the outset. Coleridge consistently enlarges upon the exquisite skill displayed by Shakespeare in building his foundations, or perhaps more properly in planting his seeds and nourishing their tender growth. For the critic there is the equivalent necessity of establishing his idea of the play, the germ that is the source of its unity.

Thus for Coleridge the germ of a Shakespearean drama is some dislocation or disproportion, something wrong and out of order, a problem that the drama must pursue and finally reconcile. In the famous analysis of *Hamlet* he speaks of

> Shakespeare's mode of conceiving characters out of his own intellectual and moral faculties, by conceiving any one intellectual or moral faculty in morbid excess and then placing himself, thus mutilated and diseased, under given circumstances. This we shall have repeated occasion to restate and enforce. In Hamlet I conceive him to have wished to exemplify the moral necessity of a due balance between our attention to outward objects and our meditation on inward thoughts—a due balance between the real and the imaginary world. In Hamlet this balance does not exist—his thoughts, images, and fancy [being] far more vivid than his perceptions, and his very perceptions instantly passing thro' the medium of his contemplations, and acquiring as they pass a form and color not naturally their own. Hence great, enormous, intellectual activity, and a consequent proportionate aversion to real action, with all its symptoms and accompanying qualities.[42]

For *Hamlet* this imbalance is the germ of both character and play, but the initial dislocation may be anything that constitutes an interesting human problem. Analysis will find in it some dominant attribute or direction, here the psychological interest of Hamlet's inwardness, but it contains potentially a world of interests which open out from it.

The drama in its totality will then be a reconciliation and a synthesis, neither strictly logical nor real, but representational and symbolic, taking for its grounds an imagined situation and imaginatively developing its meaning by the agency of the mind of the dramatic poet. Coleridge deals with a play as an organic unity, a totality of variety and unity reconciled, with almost infinitely complex interrelationships, and with the apparently unpredictable "physiognomic" individuality of life itself, yet controlled by an idea that explains all individual relationships and reconciles all apparent contradictions. The interrelations of a play range between the extremes of absolute identity and contrariety, purposefully directed in their actions and reactions toward the utmost development permitted by their nature. For Coleridge, in fact, the drama as imitation of nature partakes of the "one great principle" common to all the fine arts,

> a principle which probably is the condition of all consciousness, without which we should feel and imagine only by discontinuous moments, and be plants or animals instead of men. I mean that ever-varying balance, or balancing, of images, notions, or feelings . . . conceived as in opposition to each other; in short, the perception of identity and contrariety, the least degree of which constitutes *likeness*, the greatest absolute difference; but the infinite gradations between these two form all the play and all the interest of our intellectual and moral being, till it lead us to a feeling and an object more awful than it seems to me compatible with even the present subject to utter aloud, tho' [I am] most desirous to suggest it. For there alone are all things at once different and the same; there alone, as [in] the principle of all things, does distinction exist unaided by division —will and reason, succession of time and unmoving eternity, infinite change and ineffable rest.[43]

The "ever-varying balance, or balancing," and the "infinite gradations" between identity and contrariety demand great subtlety of their critical recorder, as well as the opposite virtue of a grasp of the whole in which they exist. Consider the "snail-horn delicacy" of Coleridge's treatment of the first scene of *Hamlet:*

> Compare the easy language of common life in which this drama opens, with the wild wayward lyric of the opening of *Macbeth.* The language is familiar: no poetic descriptions of night, no elaborate information conveyed by one speaker to another of what both had before their immediate perceptions (such as the first distich in Addison's Cato, which is a translation into poetry of "Past four o'clock, and a damp morning")—yet nothing bordering on the comic on the one hand, and no striving of the intellect on the other. It is the language of *sensation* among men who feared no charge of effeminacy for feeling what they felt no want of resolution to bear. Yet the armour, the dead silence, that watchfulness that first interrupts it, the welcome relief of guard, the cold, the broken expressions as of a man's compelled attention to bodily feelings allowed no man,—all excellently accord with and prepare for the after gradual rise into tragedy—but above all into a tragedy the interest of which is eminently *ad et apud intra,* as *Macbeth* . . . [?] is *ad extra.*
>
> The preparation informative of the audience [is] just as much as was precisely necessary: how gradual first, and with the uncertainty appertaining to a question—
>
> What, has *this thing* appeared *again* tonight.
>
> Even the word "again" has its *credibilizing* effect. Then the representative of the ignorance of the audience, Horatio (not himself but [quoted by] Marcellus to Bernardo) anticipates the common solution, " 'tis but our phantasy." But Marcellus rises secondly into "[this] dreaded sight." Then

> this "thing" becomes at once an "apparition," and that too an intelligent spirit that is to be *spoken* to
>
> Tush, tush, 'twill not appear.
>
> Then the shivery feeling, at such a time, with two eye-witnesses, of sitting down to hear a story of a ghost, and this, too, a ghost that had appeared two nights before [at] about this very time. The effort of the narrator to master his own imaginative terrors; the consequent elevation of the style, itself a continuation of this effort; the turning off to an outward object, "yon same star." O heaven! words are wasted to those that feel and to those who do not feel the exquisite judgment of Shakespeare. Hume himself could not but have faith in *this* Ghost dramatically, let his anti-ghostism be as strong as Samson against ghosts less powerfully raised.

All this is immediate preparation for the first entrance of the Ghost, a gradual rise within the "after gradual rise into tragedy," compacted of likenesses and differences, "the easy language of common life" with "the armour, the dead silence, the watchfulness" that is its opposite and counterpart, and the modulation of style to correspond with minute shiftings of the mood. After the Ghost's first appearance, Coleridge notes in Marcellus' "Good now, sit down, and tell me, he that knows," an "exquisitely natural transit into the narration retrospective." [44]

Such interpretation is almost tremblingly alive, and it is central and comprehensive. From his idea of the play, and within his pattern of developing action and reaction, Coleridge is able to utilize his own exquisite tact and his own knowledge of poetry (not to speak of his knowledge of the theater), his philosophic grasp of human nature, and his genius for introspection, intelligibly because of their foundations, and excitingly because the foundations are spacious. His method is dialectic, but not narrowly so; it allows him room for the contemplation of particulars, which he can analyze without dissecting them or detaching them from the living body of the play. His celebrated "psychological elaborations" have their own interest, but they are inseparable from his poetic and dramatic sense of the whole.

# 7

## *Christabel*

A LARGE BODY of modern literary interpretation, particularly in the United States, has followed the dialectic method of Coleridge's Shakespearean criticism, applying it not only to the drama but to lyric poetry as well, and latterly to the short story and the novel. Such critiques treat all types of literature as dramatic imitations of conflict, thematically stated, developed, and finally resolved. The method has its weaknesses and its dangers: incautiously handled, it confuses genres and makes inappropriate demands; of itself the only value it can state is dramatic appropriateness of function; employing a logical structure, it may see in its object only a logical argument, and instead of an organic development a linear and mechanical progression toward a predetermined end. Well employed, however, it has the advantage of focusing the problem with which as movement any literary work must deal, and of offering an evolving pattern in which the work's relationships may be studied.

The interpretation of *Christabel* in this chapter is an illustration, but does not presume to be an example, of this general method. It attempts a Coleridgean reconciliation of induction with principles. The requirement is sufficient system to permit of intelligible, communicable conclusions, combined with sufficient flexibility of approach. The approach, indeed, must be determined by the poem, so that the critique is a relatively abstract, discursive imitation of it, intended to expound the vital relationships that may be intuitively grasped but without exposition cannot be firmly possessed. My hope in commencing is that this task will be accomplished without mutilating or destroying the vitality the critique proposes to celebrate.

One might question the propriety, of which I myself am yet fully convinced, of using an early work such as *Christabel* to illuminate Coleridge's mature critical method and thought. Yet fundamentally Coleridge's poetry and thought, his early and his later literary life, are one and the same. This is not to blink Coleridge's apparent shifts, such as his great swing from Hartley to idealism; but I affirm here the basic consistency and continuity of Coleridge's development, considering that in his philosophy "distinction is not division," that in his mind as in his dialectic he struggled to synthesize oppositions into organic unity, with Wordsworthian confidence that nothing need finally be discarded as irrelevant or irreconcilable.

The theme of Coleridge's *Christabel* is the problem of innocence; or, framed as an opposition, it is the beauty of innocence, represented by the heroine, against the beauty of evil in the enchantress Geraldine.[1] Christabel is lovely, holy, and sheltered; the insidious Geraldine is the first evil thing in her experience. From this point of view *Christabel* might be taken for an "initiation" story, concentrating upon that crucial moment between childhood and maturity which decides the direction of the individual's further growth. Freudian and Jungian critics would find material in *Christabel,* and the methods of their depth psychology could also be applied to it. From their close relationship Christabel and Geraldine may be taken as different aspects of the same person. Thus Christabel could be interpreted as the conscious opposed to Geraldine the unconscious mind, the ego or superego to her id; or if the heroine's mother were added to the scheme as superego the scheme could be made triadic, with the mother as reconciler of the opposition or, more simply, as a means of escape or evasion.

In a kindred mythical pattern this opposition could be represented in the Uranian and the Pandemonian Aphrodite, sacred versus profane love; or, correspondingly, Agape versus Eros, or Apollo versus Dionysus. If we view Geraldine in herself, the variety of her shifts and disguises suggests the displacements and transferences of the Freudian theory of dream imagery, which would have some warrant from Coleridge's own experience. Geraldine bears some occult relation to Christabel's mother, who died in giving her birth; her proximity occasions ambiguous dreams; she may or may not be the daughter of a family friend, Lord Roland de Vaux of Tryermaine; and in Dr. Gilman's account of Coleridge's plan for finishing the poem Geraldine is to appear in the false guise of Christabel's lover. This protean quality of Geraldine's is interesting as a version of the one and the many, a single identity persisting under various forms, as Coleridge called Shakespeare the single divinity, "the one Proteus of fire and flood." This analogy is arbitrary and tenuous, but Coleridge was unquestionably preoccupied with the basic relationship that suggests the connection.

If one considers Geraldine in her influence upon Christabel, her ambiguity has symbolic import. Evil can attack the spirit in many forms, and it may be unintended by the agent in whom it is lodged. There may be evil for us in mother, friend, or lover, ambiguous but real, unwilled but inherent in being itself. This notion would serve to explain Geraldine's strange reluctance to carry out her mission, which many critics have pointed out. Although the agent she is also a victim of evil, controlled by forces she would willingly escape. It has been suggested that she is a victim of demonic possession, an idea that would make her beauty and goodness not merely apparent but real, and render her an unfortunate case of split personality. This idea is the connecting link of Mr. Nethercot's studies in vampire, lamia, and demon lore; like the vampire and the lamia Geraldine is a victim as well as a villain, and like the demon she is an unwilling emissary of unknown powers and destinies.[2]

These various possibilities are sparkles cast off by *Christabel* as one turns it in the light, and it is significant of the poem's complexity that it can evoke them. Each, however, illuminates only a single facet, and all are imposed from without, assuming structures of belief and relationship for which the poem gives no real warrant. If Geraldine, for example, is specifically a vampire, lamia, demon, or witch, Coleridge has kept his own counsel in the matter. We know that she is an evil being in the form of a beautiful woman, and the specification of her rank and regiment in the armies of darkness can only lessen her power upon imagination. Of the crucial revelation, "A sight to dream of, not to tell," E. H. Coleridge remarks that the poet's omission of detail is "on the principle of 'omne ignotum pro MYSTERIO,'"[3] and Coleridge's references to the supernatural bear this out.

If it were necessary to find a source for the supernatural elements in *Christabel*, Book I of Spenser's *Faerie Queene* would be the most interesting candidate for the honor.[4] In *Christabel* the discrepancy between appearance and reality is vitally important, for evil cannot triumph directly. It must resort for its weapons to confusion and disguise. Thus in the heroine Christabel, appearance and reality are one—Una; but in Geraldine they are two, as in the false witch Duessa, who disguises herself as the maid Fidessa. Like Una, Christabel is "holy," and we recall that Holiness is the theme of Spenser's Book I.

In *The Faerie Queene* evil must always resort to

duplicity, for in direct encounters good is stronger, and is aided not only by its spiritual powers but also by the force of chivalry and arms. The enchanter Archimago disguises himself as the Red Cross Knight, but his armor is no more than a hollow shell. Entrapped by circumstances into an open fight, he is unhorsed at the first onset by the Paynim Sansloy, in one of the many instances of mistaken identity with which *The Faerie Queene* abounds (Book I, Canto 3, 34–39). Archimago on other occasions succeeds in deceiving St. George, the Red Cross Knight, by a variety of disguises, as Geraldine deceives Christabel and Sir Leoline. He works also through false dreams, which are calculated to destroy the integrity of the dreamer whom they attack. Such are Christabel's dreams as she lies imprisoned in the arms of Geraldine. They are literally true, for she is

> Fearfully dreaming, yet, I wis,
> Dreaming that alone which is . . . ,

but in the last analysis they are delusions. *The Faerie Queene* shows the same mingling of dream and reality as *Christabel* when St. George, who has been dreaming of Una, awakes to find the apparition of Una standing by his side (Canto 1, 45–49). There is a difference, for the seeming Una is only an invention of Archimago's, whereas Christabel is awakened by the real Geraldine. Yet the resemblance remains, for Geraldine as we know her in the poem is false to begin with.

The resemblances between *The Faerie Queene* and *Christabel,* however, point to an essential distinction. Spenser's disguises and delusions are merely physical and temporary. He is careful to present before us his evil creatures as they really are, for the reader is not to share the confusions of the characters. In Coleridge the problem is deep-seated, like the ambiguity of James's "The Turn of the Screw," or of Hawthorne's "Rappaccini's Daughter," in which only heaven can separate the tangled strands of good and evil. It is clearly Coleridge's intention to provide a happy ending—

> But this she knows, in joys and woes,
> That saints will aid if men will call:
> For the blue sky bends over all!—

yet, on the other hand, Geraldine's spell, like the spell on the Ancient Mariner, is woven for the precise purpose of making Christabel unable to call for aid. Doubtless, as in *The Ancient Mariner,* the spell was to be broken—"Sure my kind saint had pity on me!"—but the poem actually leaves Christabel completely entangled.

This complexity is reflected in Geraldine herself, alike agent and victim. Whereas Spenser's characters are allegorical representations of qualities, and in themselves lifeless, Geraldine is an individual as well as an emissary, with her own self-conflicts, her revulsions as well as her unhallowed pride. On occasions she counterfeits goodness and reality so successfully that we hardly know what to think, as when, upon arising,

> . . . her looks, her air
> Such gentle thankfulness declare
> That (so it seemed) her girded vests
> Grew tight beneath her heaving breasts.

One explanation, of course, is simply that Coleridge is inordinately skillful in working up suspense, but the problem goes beyond the technical requirements of the genre.

For Coleridge the poem of the supernatural is comparable within its kind to the "Romantic drama," and shares with it the ultimate purpose of enlivening our perceptions, awakening our affections, and increasing our ability to imagine reality.[5] It must defeat the prejudices and prepossessions of the understanding, which is bounded by the senses and the abstract logic derived from them. This victory is to be won, however, not by literally taking leave of the senses but by limiting them to their proper sphere. The poem of the supernatural is, like other works of the imagination, a reconciliation of understanding and reason, though with a greater than usual freedom from the bounds of time and space in accordance with its emphasis and function. It intends to endow with provisional reality a supersensuous world, through the concrete, sensuous medium of art.

Correspondingly the illusion that is the immediate artistic end of the poem of the supernatural is a mean between delusion and literal reality. Here it is necessary to distinguish with extreme care, in order to convey the precise nuance of meaning in the famous phrase, "the willing suspension of disbelief." The formula provides a way of distinguishing poetry, the discourse of imagination, from religion, science, and philosophy, by avoiding the terms of truth and belief in connection with it. Religion, philosophy, science, history all try to equip us to deal directly with reality, and in order to do so they abstract from it, whereas poetry as an imitation proposes to help us grasp as much reality as we can in the imagination. Reality is the imagination of God, whereas poetry and art are the imagination of man. We cannot possibly imagine too much, so that after its kind the poem of the supernatural is the truest realism, which enlarges our minds to a true vision of the infinite creation. Only we must not confuse imaginative creation with literal belief, when we are confronted with matters beyond our literal knowledge. Supernatural beings are by definition beyond us.

Thus Coleridge believes in supernatural powers, and infers from all he knows of the natural world a supernatural hierarchy between ourselves and God. But he cannot present the figures of imagination as figures of literal truth. Ideas, in his sense of the term, are always indefinite, and can be comprehended only when embodied in symbols, not when fixed, as in allegory, to represent something already determined and known. A supernatural character such as Geraldine is a symbol of spiritual conflict and evil, and in that sense she is real; but we do not learn of her real form, which remains ambiguous, and we are not entitled to draw up a system of supernatural Mammalia in which she can be accurately classified as vampire, lamia, or witch-woman. She is not, on the other hand, merely a means of expressing psychological conflicts,[6] such as Coleridge's own inner stresses at the time of writing, although these as well as his knowledge of demon lore may very well have entered into her total composition. Coleridge's psychology should never be divorced from his cosmos of nature and spirit; he is always looking outward and upward as well as inside. The mental faculties of his psychological vocabulary belong to his philosophy and to his criticism as well, and even to his theology; they are organs of knowledge, not merely peepholes for watching the mind's behavior.

E. H. Coleridge comments finely upon the beginning of *Christabel,* that crucial sector of the poem of the supernatural where acquiescence and sympathy must primarily be won:

> Perhaps the most wonderful quality or characteristic of this First Part . . . is that the action is not that of a drama which is *ex hypothesi* a representative of fact;—nor are we persuaded to reproduce it for ourselves as by a tale that is told, but we behold it, scene after scene, episode by episode, as in a mirror, as the Lady of Shalott saw the knights ride by. If we stay to think of Christabel "praying beneath the huge oak tree" or of Geraldine and Christabel crossing the moat and passing through the hall, and stealing their way from stair to stair, our minds make pictures, but we do not stay to think or reflect on their fears or their rejoicings. We "see, we see it all," and now in glimmer and now in gloom we "live o'er again" that midnight hour. It is not a tale that is told, it is a personal experience. The mechanism which shifts the scenes is worked by nature and not by art. The necessity of their connexion is not logical,

but in the strictest sense of the word, accidental. It happened, and it was so.[7]

E. H. C. catches the effect of *Christabel* admirably, and he goes on to praise its artistry. His account is, however, metaphorical, and perhaps occasionally misleading. Do we see the scenes of Part I "as in a mirror"? Perhaps, if the mirror is an idealizing and selective medium like the dim moonlight that picks out the early scenes; otherwise, the figure might be thought ill-chosen. It would be better to say that they appear before us suddenly as if by magic, with the magician sometimes visibly directing our attention from close by, and sometimes orally expressing them in broken exclamations or lulling musical cadences. And in what sense we see the scenes is questionable, as indeed E. H. C. appears to hint. It may be idiosyncrasy, but I do not really visualize the "huge, broad-breasted, old oak tree," or Christabel, or Geraldine, nor am I prompted to do so. I imagine outlines, a vague silhouette of the tree, and attitudes, like Christabel praying, or Christabel and Geraldine stealing toward the castle; I catch the shadowy gleam of Geraldine's robe, and the glitter of the jewels in her hair. By his skillful use of a few particulars, Coleridge convinces us that the scene exists and could be described if it were desirable to do so; and this is enough to secure the suspension of our disbelief and render us receptive, to convince us that here is a mystery worth straining to illumine. We recall that Coleridge was skeptical about detailed description in poetry, and relegated it to the fancy. It is a law of the imagination to create living wholes out of parts, if the parts have the potentiality of life.

The effect of immediacy so necessary to the supernatural is also attained by a kind of hypnotism. The poet acts as an Ancient Mariner to the reader's Wedding Guest. This hypnotic quality is partly suggested by the subject matter. To talk of trances, dreams, spells, and of the hypnotic power of the eye, is a step toward inducing their effects, and Coleridge accompanies the narrative with the equivalent of dramatic gesture and recitation in his meter and melody. Like the rhapsode Ion he intends, although more subtly, to raise up absent things as though they were present. He makes use of emotional notations both direct and indirect, as in the sudden, ostensibly involuntary exclamation, "O shield her! shield sweet Christabel!" or the quieter comment on Geraldine,

> She was most beautiful to see
> Like a lady of a far countrie.

The poet has a steady sense of his audience, and an eye for both his matter and his manner. To win us he must himself be captivated ("himself that great Sublime he draws"), and also be able to infect us with his feelings by his power of projecting them upon us. To achieve his effect, however, he needs to make use of variety. In a poem of any length it is impossible to maintain an even intensity throughout, or to keep precisely equidistant from one's material. Thus Coleridge steadily alternates, for example, between the present as his narrative tense and the somewhat more distant past, not with mechanical regularity but so constantly that the usage must have been intended. By itself the historical present would after a certain point be mannered and unnatural; the variation tempers it while it supports its effect.

The supernatural poem must assert, not argue. It presents a necessity without logic, and it would be fatal to protest too much. Therefore its opening is characteristically swift:

> 'Tis the middle of night by the castle clock,
> And the owls have awakened the crowing
> cock;
> Tu—whit! ——Tu—whoo!
> And hark, again! the crowing cock,
> How drowsily it crew.

It is worthwhile noting for its bearing upon Coleridge's method in *Christabel* that line 3 is direct dramatic presentation, with stage directions added in lines 4–5, and to some degree in the spelling and punctuation. The single and double dashes and the extra *o* indicate extraordinary duration, as does the same usage in lines 306–310, dramatically appropriate in its context:

By tairn and rill,
The night-birds all that hour were still.
But now they are jubilant anew,
From cliff and tower, tu—whoo! tu—whoo!
Tu—whoo! tu—whoo! from wood and fell!

The continued repetitions suggest that echoes and reverberations fill all the interspaces and intensify until the point of danger at which one's ear begins to rebel.

Coleridge's description reconciles particularity with sparseness. It is precise without being in the least luxuriant. The poet is exact almost to grotesqueness (possibly as an antidote to the danger of bathos) in the "Sixteen short howls, not over loud" (l. 12) of the mastiff, in the observation that "The night is chilly, but not dark" (l. 15), and in the statement that

The thin gray cloud is spread on high,
It covers but not hides the sky. [Ll. 16–17.]

The old oak tree is bare save for "moss and rarest mistletoe" (l. 34) and the famous "one red leaf, the last of its clan" (l. 49). Most striking, perhaps, is the effect of the cloud covering upon the moon:

The moon is behind, and at the full;
And yet she looks both small and dull.
[Ll. 18–19.]

More incidentally, it might be remarked that the two daring rhetorical questions ("Is the night chilly and dark?" and "Is it the wind that moaneth bleak?") on the one hand focus and project the scene toward the foreground, and on the other modify the impression of it by their incantatory quality, which tends to formalize it.

The imagery of Part I, then, endows the scenes with a life of their own. Sparse as it is, it possesses the mingled delicacy and fullness that are characteristic of Coleridge's sensibility. Everything is modulated. The cock that is awakened by the owls crows drowsily, the howls of the mastiff are not overloud, the night is chilly but not dark, and "The moon shines dim in the open air" (l. 175). These touches serve the genre of the supernatural, with a vitality added from Coleridge's own nature. A good deal remains to be said, however, of the bearing of the imagery upon the themes and motifs of *Christabel,* and in turn of their functions in the service of the meaning as a whole.

The technical function of the references to trance and dream has been mentioned. They help to establish the suspension of everyday judgment which is common both to dream and to the atmosphere of the poem of the supernatural. Dreams and trance states, however, as expressions of the inner, subterranean reality of the unconscious mind, also raise a crucial problem of meaning. Where is truth to be found, in the dream or in the waking? "Fled is that music,—do I wake or sleep?" asks Keats, and does not answer. And what is the relationship between the two? For there are waking dreams in *Christabel,* and it is not easy to keep the two states clearly separate. Dreams seem to be both good and evil, too: Christabel's prayer beneath the oak tree is a kind of dreaming in its concentrated devotion, associated with dreams "Of her own betrothed knight," and this impression is reinforced by the reprise at the conclusion to Part I:

> Kneeling in the moonlight
> To make her gentle vows;
> Her slender palms together prest,
> Heaving sometimes on her breast;
> Her face resigned to bliss or bale.
>
> [Ll. 284–288.]

The conclusion goes on to make an explicit contrast with another waking dream, this time of evil:

With open eyes (ah woe is me!)
Asleep, and dreaming fearfully,
Fearfully dreaming, yet, I wis,
Dreaming that alone, which is—
O sorrow and shame! Can this be she,
The lady, who knelt at the old oak tree?
[Ll. 292–297.]

Meanwhile, in a strange reversal of values,

And lo! the worker of these harms,
That holds the maiden in her arms,
Seems to slumber still and mild,
As a mother with her child. [Ll. 298–301.]

The juxtaposition of Geraldine and the mother is horrible and perverse, yet in Christabel's dream the two must somehow be united, for the image of mother and child merges with another dream, this time beneficent. Christabel "Gathers herself from out her trance," and

Her limbs relax, her countenance
Grows sad and soft; the smooth thin lids
Close o'er her eyes; and tears she sheds—
Large tears that leave the lashes bright!
And oft the while she seems to smile
As infants at a sudden light! [Ll. 312–318.]

The effect is to add to the complexity of the situation. In some occult sense the enchantress Geraldine and Christabel's mother, "her guardian spirit," are one and the same.

In Part II Christabel is again cast into a trance at the sight of Geraldine, once more beautiful after the terrible revelations of the night just passed, in the welcoming embrace of her father Sir Leoline. She is overwhelmed by the ironic contrast:

Which when she viewed, a vision fell
Upon the soul of Christabel,
The vision of fear, the touch and pain!
She shrunk, and shuddered, and saw
again—
(Ah, woe is me! Was it for thee,

Thou gentle maid! such sights to see?)
Again she saw that bosom old,
Again she felt that bosom cold,
And drew in her breath with a hissing sound:
Whereat the Knight turned wildly round,
And nothing saw, but his own sweet maid
With eyes upraised, as one that prayed.

[Ll. 451–462.]

Again the vision of evil passes swiftly into its opposite, the "vision Blest" of the mother, and again the connection between the mother and Geraldine is placed before us, supported by the remark that Geraldine is in outward appearance "a thing divine." From a different point of view this remark is merely one link in the chain of ironies in which Christabel is helplessly bound throughout the poem, beginning from the moment she innocently places herself within the power of evil; and from this point of view the reference to Geraldine's divinity serves to heighten the contrast between appearance and reality. Yet the possibility remains that the mother and Geraldine are, for Christabel, somehow one.

Bard Bracy's dream vision, which follows, symbolizes the plight of Christabel as a dove coiled about by a snake:

So strange a dream hath come to me,
That I had vowed with music loud
To clear yon wood from thing unblest,
Warned by a vision in my rest!

[Ll. 527–530.]

Then Christabel undergoes the same trance experience as before, narrated in terms of the snake image suggested by Bracy's account of his dream. This time, however, she undergoes not the shock of ironic contrast, as before, but the direct shock of Geraldine's malice and power: [8]

At Christabel she looked askance!—
One moment—and the sight was fled!

But Christabel in dizzy trance
Stumbling on the unsteady ground
Shuddered aloud, with a hissing sound;
And Geraldine again turned round,
And like a thing, that sought relief,
Full of wonder and full of grief,
She rolled her large bright eyes divine
Wildly on Sir Leoline. [Ll. 587–596.]

Once again Geraldine becomes almost instantly a thing divine. At this penultimate moment of the poem, however, Christabel is terribly isolated and estranged from her entire moral and social world, as if by the trance that has torn her away. She reflects the evil that has come upon her in a "look of dull and treacherous hate." The trance passes, and she regains a measure of self-possession, but what she can reveal is fatally misunderstood, as it is in a literal sense fatally liable to misunderstanding:

And when the trance was o'er the maid
Paused awhile, and inly prayed:
Then falling at the Baron's feet,
"By my mother's soul do I entreat
That thou this woman send away!"
She said: and more she could not say:
For what she knew she could not tell,
O'er-mastered by the mighty spell.
[Ll. 613–620.]

The prayer "By my mother's soul," however, once more links Geraldine and the mother in an ambiguous association.

Imagery of bareness enters into the dream-and-trance theme, as a question of reality. As *Christabel* is a drama of concealment, revelation is a matter of some importance. What is revealed is of course ugly and fearsome, and one has some ominous hint of a hidden death that lies at the root of things. Coleridge has chosen a cold and bare forest for his opening scene, with no life except the parasite moss and mistletoe, and no movement except the weird dance of "The one red leaf, the last of its clan." It is in this setting of chill and death, half-lighted by a dull moon, that the evil thing comes forth. Christabel bares her feet (l. 166) in an ironic effect of concealment, as she and her dangerous guest steal silently through the castle; and Geraldine bids her to "unrobe yourself" (l. 233) under the pretext that she in the meantime must pray. But Christabel lies down "in her loveliness," having nothing to hide; what she is and what she pretends to be are the same. The central event of the poem is of course the revelation of Geraldine—"Behold! her bosom and half her side" [9]—as she, with a strange reluctance, unbinds "The cincture from beneath her breast," and allows her gown to drop to the floor. What she unbares is evidently ugly and shameful to herself as well as to the horrified beholder, but the only concrete hint of its nature has to be learned retrospectively from the unhappy trance vision of Christabel in Part II:

> Again she saw that bosom old,
> Again she felt that bosom cold. . . .
>
> [Ll. 457–458.]

When she dresses herself in the morning Geraldine apparently puts on youth, beauty, and goodness with her gown:

> Puts on her silken vestments white,
> And tricks her hair in lovely plight
> . . . . . . . .
> And while she spake, her looks, her air
> Such gentle thankfulness declare,
> That (so it seemed) her girded vests
> Grew tight beneath her heaving breasts.
>
> [Ll. 364–365, 377–380.]

A little earlier in this discussion I raised the question: Might not this goodness and beauty in a sense be genuine? It is not the prerogative of the critic to answer, and hardly within the power of the poet.

Images of the eye and of the serpent in *Christabel*

are closely linked with the themes of dream and of revelation, and they are inevitably joined to each other by the notion of the snake's hypnotic eye. The small, dull moon of the opening scene comes, we know, from observation, on the evidence of Dorothy Wordsworth's journal; but it takes on symbolic meaning as an ominous eye when we compare it with later indications in the poem. The mastiff, which "Lay fast asleep in moonshine cold," moans angrily as Christabel and Geraldine pass by her, and it is said pointedly that

> Never till now she uttered yell
> Beneath the eye of Christabel.
> [Ll. 150–151.]

Beneath the eye of Christabel, no; but another eye is to be considered. Shortly after, in the midst of the mounting series of premonitory warnings that an evil spirit is present, a sudden tongue of light from the fire flares up,

> And Christabel saw the lady's eye,
> And nothing else saw she thereby,
> Save the boss of the shield of Sir Leoline tall,
> Which hung in a murky old niche in the wall. [Ll. 160–163.]

The boss of the shield is another eye, a silent evidence that the castle is somehow awake and watchful. If one observes the several uses of the word "shield" throughout the poem, this detail deepens in meaning.

Geraldine's eyes receive special attention, and their aspect as Geraldine is serpent or beautiful woman is directly in contrast; the blue eyes of Christabel are also contrasted with them. The enchantress stares "with unsettled eye" (l. 208) when by a false step she has evoked the presence of her victim's guardian spirit, whereas Christabel in astonished sympathy

> . . . knelt by the lady's side
> And raised to heaven her eyes so blue.
> [Ll. 214–215.]

Recovering herself, in one of the many alternations of the poem, Geraldine rises, and "Her fair large eyes 'gan glitter bright" (l. 221). The "glitter" is an echo of the glitter of her jewels in the moonlight (l. 64), which glitter *wildly*. Geraldine's eyes are unnaturally large, bright, and wild, in direct contrast with their smallness and dullness in her other aspect. Excess in one direction prepares us for excess in the other, according to Coleridge's dictum that "extremes meet." Thus during the central episodes of the eye in Part II Geraldine's eyes are the eyes of a snake, and she is a serpent in physical attitude, whereas both before and afterward her eyes are large and bright, and she is a stately and beautiful woman who looks in appeal to the Baron:

> And Geraldine in maiden wise
> Casting down her large bright eyes,
> With blushing cheek and courtesy fine
> She turned her from Sir Leoline;
> Softly gathering up her train,
> That o'er her right arm fell again;
> And folded her arms across her chest,
> And couched her head upon her breast,
> And looked askance at Christabel—
> Jesu, Maria, shield her well!
>
> A snake's small eye blinks dull and shy
> And the lady's eyes they shrunk in her head,
> Each shrunk up to a serpent's eye,
> And with somewhat of malice, and more
> of dread,
> At Christabel she looked askance!—
> One moment—and the sight was fled!
> But Christabel in dizzy trance
> Stumbling on the unsteady ground
> Shuddered aloud, with a hissing sound;
> And Geraldine again turned round,

And like a thing, that sought relief,
Full of wonder and full of grief,
She rolled her large bright eyes divine
Wildly on Sir Leoline. [Ll. 573–596.]

There is perhaps more appropriateness in the familiar anecdote of Shelley and *Christabel* than we ordinarily consider. It will be recalled that he imagined Geraldine with eyes where nipples should have been.

Christabel's blue eyes are heavenly, akin to the blue sky that "bends over all." During her prayer beneath the oak they are "more bright than clear" with unshed tears of devotion (ll. 290–291). They are fearfully open in her enthrallment to Geraldine; when she is recovered and naturally asleep, her lids close (perhaps an oblique allusion to the serpent's lidless eyes), and she weeps and smiles at once (ll. 314–318). Sir Leoline's eyes are also expressive, although they always express a misunderstanding of the meaning of what is going on; the boss of his shield, in fact, shows insight superior to his. His first vision of Geraldine fills them with "cheerful wonder" (l. 399); "his eye in lightning rolls" (l. 444) at her supposed wrongs; later they are "made up of wonder and love" (l. 567) in admiration of her; "his eyes were wild" (l. 641) at Christabel's apparent breach of hospitality to their guest; and finally "He rolled his eye with stern regard" (l. 648) upon Bracy, as he orders him away from the unhappy scene.

The serpent motif, intermingled as it is with the other themes, appears by itself in Bracy's dream vision of the dove and the snake:

I stooped, methought, the dove to take,
When lo! I saw a bright green snake
Coiled around its wings and neck.
Green as the herbs on which it couched,
Close by the dove's its head it crouched;
And with the dove it heaves and stirs,
Swelling its neck as she swelled hers!
[Ll. 548–554.]

Like Geraldine the snake disguises itself, taking on the coloration of its background, and like Geraldine it holds its victim in physical embrace. Color is used sparingly in *Christabel,* with a lightly stressed symbolic value. Green, the color of universal nature, occurs only unnaturally, in parasitic moss and mistletoe among the bare forest trees, until Bracy's vision, where it is modified into the "bright lady" Geraldine. Its suggestions are therefore perverse. In the snake-Geraldine conjunction the serpent's bright green is analogous to her shining white robe and her dazzling skin, which counterfeit the holiness of Christabel and her mother and her guardian saint. The color for Christabel, partly no doubt through a principle of emphasis and variety which would deny to her the use of white, is the heavenly but warmer and less assuming blue, proper to the sky and to the Virgin Mary. To return to the snake theme, Geraldine's voice is reported as "faint and sweet" (ll. 72, 76) in preparation for the contrast of the "hissing sound" (ll. 459, 591) that the unfortunate Christabel under her influence twice utters involuntarily. Another such irony occurs in Sir Leoline's promise to Geraldine (l. 571) that "Thy sire and I will crush the snake!"

The snake theme must stand in the center of any interpretation of *Christabel.* In a sense interpretation is impossible—matter-of-factly, because the poem is unfinished, and more fundamentally, because no abstraction can comprise within itself the poem's potentialities of meaning. Coleridge has refrained from attempting to say what he means, and his doctrine of symbol should warn us to leave his meanings embedded in their substance, inseparable from its life and being. One may, however, legitimately discuss his symbols' capability to suggest. It is almost certain, as Nethercot declares, that there is something of the lamia in Geraldine, but perhaps a more orthodox snake, "the old serpent" [10] of the Garden of Eden, will provide a more interesting background for her. One thinks especially of the Satan of *Paradise Lost,* that bright and ruined archangel, with his disguises as serpent and toad; and also of the universal hiss as Satan and his peers receive the reward of their triumph in Pandemonium.

*Christabel* is, indeed, after its kind a story of the Fall of Man. It is not the story of the original Fall, with its problems of predestination and free will, but of the consequences of the Fall for every mortal. Christabel does not sin, but she is liable for her human debt. In this regard *Christabel* is more like Blake's *Book of Thel* than like *Paradise Lost.* It is the first encounter of innocence with a fallen world, an event that is inevitable. Blake's attitude is of course quite different from Coleridge's: Thel has her choice of actions, and flees once more into the safe valleys of Har. In any rational sense Christabel ("The maid, devoid of guile and sin") is sinless. She is like Melville's Handsome Sailor, Billy Budd, who falls only because of the slight stammer, a symbol of the inarticulateness that is his single mortal blemish. *Christabel* is a story of the spiritual estrangement that every human being must undergo, and which swallows some of us forever. Geraldine, who so artfully insinuates herself into the castle and into the hearts of its inmates, is simply that which in one form or another must come to us all. It would be interesting to ask, concerning *Christabel,* to what extent the carelessness of innocence itself invites the evil within its doors, assuming that evil cannot initiate action. Undoubtedly, however, the conclusion Coleridge envisaged would have supposed a guardian of genuine innocence as inevitable as the evil that besets it, in the person of the dead mother. The presence of Geraldine, indeed, almost immediately evokes the mother's presence as well (ll. 202–213).

One might speculate that Coleridge was dealing, in the character of Christabel, especially with the problem of a child. Some of the images in the poem are related to observations on Hartley Coleridge in notebooks and letters, and Coleridge's feeling for young children was always strong. A child is peculiarly innocent and vulnerable, and helplessly incapable of expressing his real feelings to his elders. There are vast gulfs of misunderstanding yawning between the child and the adult, and these are perhaps invisible to the parties on either side of them. The advent of Geraldine with her "mighty spell" could be taken as a projection of the feelings of a child, suddenly and mysteriously estranged from his safe, familiar surroundings and his intimates, with no power of putting an end to his misery, and no conception that it is other than endless in itself. Every effort to escape only increases the involvement.

Christabel is of course a young woman, old enough to be married, so that such an interpretation is admittedly partial. But she is set before us as the child of her mother and Sir Leoline, and the emphasis upon her childhood seems too steady to be accidental. Geraldine holds her in her arms "As a mother with her child" (ll. 299–301) during the fatal hour of the spell. The spell relaxed, Christabel "seems to smile / As infants at a sudden light"—a reminiscence of Hartley. Sir Leoline thinks of Geraldine primarily as "the child of his friend" (l. 446), Lord Roland de Vaux of Tryermaine. The vision of the guardian saint spreads "smiles like light" upon Christabel's lips and eyes, and the Baron enquires, "What ails then my beloved child?" (Ll. 463–470.) Sir Leoline is besought repeatedly to think no evil of his child (ll. 622, 627, 634); he is especially wounded, on the other hand, to find "his only child" dishonoring him with gross inhospitality to the distressed daughter of his friend.

In *Christabel* the background of the child is a chivalric order. This setting is doubtless a "Gothic" convention—the supernatural melodrama laid in an isolated castle, at some unspecified but picturesque time in the past—but it is not merely a convention or a device of atmosphere. The strong castle and the knightly order are meant to be taken seriously, as a solid framework of values. Christabel, the holy maid, is supported by a combination of spiritual, temporal, and even (in Bracy) bardic powers, in a single cohesive society, symbolically focused in the castle, which is comparable to the encircling walls and towers of *Kubla Khan*, and the harbor, kirk, and "steady weathercock" of *The Ancient Mariner*. She is shielded by "Jesu, Maria," her guardian spirit, her baronial father, and all the forces at his command. Sir Leoline and the absent but ringingly denominated Lord Roland de Vaux of Tryermaine [11] are evidently towers of strength.

Within the walls of the castle Christabel, we imagine, is safe, but inevitably she must at some time emerge from them and take her chances as an individual in this dark and confusing world. Her purpose in venturing forth is worthy, and it is in keeping with chivalry and her society, for she intends to pray for the welfare of "her own betrothed knight." But the question is asked,

> What makes her in the wood so late,
> A furlong from the castle gate?
>
> [Ll. 26–27.]

With the implication that she has ventured outside the pale and is appropriately exposed to the evil awaiting her on the other side of the great oak, itself a symbol of strength and refuge. Threatened, her first utterance is significantly, "Mary, mother, save me now!" And Geraldine effectively disguises herself in the ceremonial robes of chivalry, as a lady outraged by wanton violation of the laws of knighthood in the persons of the mysterious "Five warriors."

Christabel comforts the supposed daughter of a noble line by offering her the service of her father Sir Leoline and "our stout chivalry." In passing the formidable entrance to the castle with the purpose of penetrating to its innermost sanctum, the bedroom of Christabel, in triumphant desecration, Geraldine has to be helped by someone from within the stronghold. Inside, the shield sternly acknowledges her presence; and Sir Leoline, as the center of the castle's power, must be evaded by stealth, although literally the furtiveness of the movement comes from consideration for his sleep. Sir Leoline's response to Geraldine's story is thoroughly chivalric:

> He swore by the wounds in Jesu's side
> He would proclaim it far and wide,
> With trump and solemn heraldry,
> That they, who thus had wronged the dame,
> Were base as spotted infamy!
> "And if they dare deny the same,
> My herald shall appoint a week,
> And let the recreant traitors seek
> My tourney court—that there and then
> I may dislodge their reptile souls
> From the bodies and the forms of men!"
>
> [Ll. 433–443.]

There is a touch of irony in "reptile souls"; the worthy Baron is doomed to look for his snakes in the wrong places. Thus, after planning on a grand scale a chivalric meeting with his friend and Geraldine's supposed father Sir Roland de Vaux, at which both nobles are to appear "with all their numerous array," he asserts confidently that

> With arms more strong than harp or song,
> Thy sire and I will crush the snake!
>
> [Ll. 570–571.]

One is tempted to speculate on the place of "harp and song" in this close-knit feudal order. Bard Bracy clearly has an integral and honorable part in it; the solemn ceremonial visit to Lord Roland is entrusted to him (ll. 483–504) as ambassador. His position is subordinate, however; his advice is disregarded and his superior insight remains unused. He alone in his dream vision has detected the evil that has crept within, although it could be pointed out that he has seen it in strictly poetic—that is, figurative and symbolic—guise: not, indeed, the tale of a cock and a bull, as the Baron evidently thinks it, but of a snake and a bird. The relation between poetry and action is fated to be indirect. Nevertheless, his powers seem almost vatic. His "music strong and saintly song" is capable of exorcising the evil thing, if the Baron would permit him to employ it for the purpose. It would be possible to take Bracy as a symbol of the romantic poet.

The meaning of *Christabel* is inseparable from its unique metrical effects. In his Preface to the poem Coleridge said that

> the metre of Christabel is not properly speaking, irregular, though it may seem so from its being founded on a new principle: namely, that of counting in each line the accents, not the syllables. Though the latter may vary from seven to twelve, yet in each line the accents will be found to be only four. Nevertheless, this occasional variation in number of syllables is not introduced wantonly, or for the mere ends of convenience, but in correspondence with some transition in the nature of the imagery or passion.

Whether the principle of *Christabel's* versification is absolutely new it would be useless, in fact mischievous, to inquire; [12] but it is highly original and entirely organic to the poem. It is evident enough that Coleridge, as his last sentence implies, was seeking after a more intimate interpenetration of meter and meaning than he believed had been hitherto accomplished.

In so doing he was also in search of variety and flexibility, to the end of dramatic expressiveness or propriety, in a complex narrative poem in which constant shifts of feeling or "passion" were to be the rule. If, however, dramatic propriety had been his only consideration he might well have chosen blank verse for his measure. There would be a number of more or less obvious reasons against such a choice. First, the genre of the supernatural presumably calls for something different; its special illusion, and the range of feeling natural to it, narrower yet more intense than in drama, would demand a more concentrated, a denser texture of metric and sound. Drama, too, has spectacle to complete it, for which the narrative poet must substitute an equivalent attraction in the verse itself. A poem, said Coleridge, should offer as much pleasure in each part as is consonant with our pleasure in it as a whole; and the poem's part-whole relationship is unique.

Thus the meter of a poem like *Christabel* exists more completely for and in itself than would the meter of any poetic drama. The meter of *Christabel* also exists more intensely in its own right than, say, that of a narrative poem by Scott or Byron, both of whom owed a debt to *Christabel* for metrical suggestions. Yet it is at the same time more organic and less arbitrary than the meters of Scott or Byron; it is more thoroughly entwined in the total meaning and the movement of the poem. It illustrates and substantiates, indeed, what Coleridge meant by the principle of individuation in his theory of life and organic unity: that, organic life being presupposed, intense individuality in a part is not only reconcilable with but essential to a corresponding intensity of the whole. The greatest variety is also the greatest unity, in the presence of a sufficient creative agency. *Christabel* cannot be termed an organic unity in the sense of a complete correspondence of idea and execution, or of a perfect reconciliation of part and whole, but its potentialities toward unity are magnificent.

The intensity of its parts is too great for its proportions. *Christabel* is Coleridge's chief poetic trial of strength, in which his strength was inadequate to the delicacy, the elaboration, and the density of texture required in the execution. The more austere among our critics have sometimes treated the author of *Christabel* as if he had been a lazy schoolboy who failed to complete his assignment in English composition. The task, however, was self-assigned, and almost impossibly exacting.

*Christabel* was evidently to be a poem in which the parts would be uniquely self-significant and consummately wrought, each part a whole in itself and yet contributing to the larger whole. If one considers first the metrical lines as the basic units, and the poetic vitality that has been lavished upon them; then the verse paragraphs, each of which is a whole, elaborated and rounded, individual and self-justifying as a stanza need not be, for no two paragraphs are exactly alike; then the conclusions to the parts, which recapitulate yet advance the argument (the conclusion to Part I is its capstone, a triadic reconciliation of opposites); [13] then the relation of Parts I and II, maintaining the same illusion and atmosphere under different conditions, one cannot wonder that Coleridge failed in his gigantic effort at infusing an unprecedented intensity of life at once into each part and into a highly complex totality. In the latter years of his life he maintained that he still had and always had had the idea of *Christabel* in mind.[14]

Coleridge apparently intended in the meter of *Christabel* a new blend of variety with unity, of flexibility with regularity. His principle of accentuation does not seem to be absolute and exclusive, as indeed we should not expect from his general habit of thought. He was too well trained in classical metrics to write lines that could not be scanned into feet, and too naturally melodious to dally with deliberate harshness or with any radical experiments in counterpoint. His meter may be analyzed as a basic iambic tetrameter with an unprecedented number of exceptions, consisting of inversions of stress or accent, and of three-syllable feet with their characteristic swiftness of movement.

Time or duration plays a large part, however. We may assume that lines with less than the average number of syllables in *Christabel* usually take more than the average time per syllable, so that they roughly equal other lines in their length. This, however, though substantially true, is not literally and arithmetically true.[15] The most important consideration is the melody. There seems to be little doubt that Coleridge intends a very wide variation in the length of time a syllable can be held; that his accents are like musical beats; [16] that his sound effects include differences of pitch and intensity or volume; and that in general he seeks freedom and variety more usual in music than in verse, as one might indicate in notations like allegro, or legato, or andante.

The verse of *Christabel* sings and, in its use of repetition, dances as well, in a ritual celebration of design which goes beyond the bounds of dramatic propriety, unless we interpret very broadly what is proper to the illusion of the supernatural. Coleridge does not of course violate propriety, which is indeed his first consideration, but he characteristically endows his meter with qualities of its own, and his parts with their own vitality. Thus there is the dance of the leaf:

> There is not wind enough to twirl
> The one red leaf, the last of its clan,
> That dances as often as dance it can,
> Hanging so light, and hanging so high
> On the topmost twig that looks up at the
> sky. [Ll. 48–52.]

The image functions in its context to suggest the dead bareness of the forest trees, and, by an interesting contrast, to convey the stillness of the air. But the passage also stands by itself as a *danse macabre,* at once wailing and exultant in singing and dancing. The song, one might say, commences with the lilting ripple from the extra syllable of "The one red leaf, the last of its clan"; the dance begins in the words and the beat of the following line, and there is a movement of vertiginous swinging in the parallelism of "Hanging so light, and hanging so high," with height, distance, and piercing melancholy and joy combined, from the interfusion of the vowel quality in *light* and *high* with the movement of the line and the meanings of the words.

A semihypnotic incantation is no doubt the principal effect, as in Geraldine's "In the touch of this bosom there worketh a spell . . ." (ll. 267–278), and in Sir Leoline's orders to the Bard, which he imagines executed even while uttering

> (And when he has crossed the Irthing flood,
> My merry bard! he hastes, he hastes . . .),

so that they seem to be accompanied by the movements of an actor. In each instance, however, there is a self-delighting power of pure aesthetic design which goes beyond the function of meaning in even its broadest sense: in the excursions and the returns of the balladlike repetitions and refrains, and in the variations of couplets, the more fluid cross rhyming, and the occasional mounting triplets. Repetition, on the order of the Miltonic turn, is a characteristic of *Christabel*.[17] It occurs in sound, or in syllable, as in internal rhyme, in words and phrases, and more elaborately in complete sentences. It is a device of vital progression which is basic to Coleridge and peculiarly typical of *Christabel*'s elaborate technique, a single configuration of the winding filaments of growth, the never-ceasing play of associations that represent Coleridge's idea of organic unity.[18]

This critique of *Christabel* is the furthest extension of Coleridge's critical principles to be attempted in my study, and it may be thought to strain the limits of literalism in application. This freedom is, I trust, forgivable as itself essentially Coleridgean, and consonant with the spirit of genial criticism. In earlier chapters I have sought to convey the "idea" of Coleridge as critic in a dual sense, on the one hand by laying bare his central concepts, on the other by interpreting "idea" Platonically as "ideal," imagining his criticism as the totally realized unit that of course it literally is not. Coleridge's contribution as a critic may never be definitively assessed, as his criticism is formally incomplete and as the issue of plagiarism will doubtless remain a stumbling block to a proportion of serious scholars in each generation. Although respecting the sincere and grounded convictions of others, I myself have found Coleridge essentially original and consistent, and inexhaustibly suggestive, a critic unique in his powers of synthesis, sensitive in his practice, and vitally signficant now as in his own time. This "idea" of Coleridge's criticism I have also tried to present in these pages.

# *Notes*

For a list of the numerous works on Coleridge's criticism see René Wellek, "Coleridge's Philosophy and Criticism," in *The English Romantic Poets: A Review of Research*, ed. T. M. Raysor (rev. ed.; New York, Modern Language Association of America, 1956), pp. 110–137; and Wellek, *A History of Modern Criticism* (New Haven, Yale University Press, 1955), II, 388–390. I have found especially valuable James V. Baker, *The Sacred River* (Baton Rouge, Louisiana State University Press, 1957); D. G. James, *The Romantic Comedy* (London, Oxford University Press, 1948), and *Skepticism and Poetry* (London, Allen and Unwin, 1937); Gordon McKenzie, *Organic Unity in Coleridge* (Berkeley, University of California Press, 1939); Kenneth Millar, "The Inward Eye: A Revaluation of Coleridge's Psychological Criticism" (unpublished Ph.D. dissertation, University of Michigan, 1951); John H. Muirhead, *Coleridge as Philosopher* (New York, Macmillan, 1930); I. A. Richards, *Coleridge on Imagination* (New York, W. W. Norton, 1950); John Shawcross, Introduction to Vol. I, *Biographia Literaria* (2 vols.; Oxford, Clarendon Press, 1907); C. D. Thorpe, "Coleridge as Aesthetician and Critic," *Journal of the History of Ideas*, V (1944), 387–414; Basil Willey, *Nineteenth Century Studies: Coleridge to Matthew Arnold* (New York, Columbia University Press, 1949); and M. H. Abrams, *The Mirror and the Lamp* (New York, Oxford University Press, 1953).

## CHAPTER 1.

[1] Coleridge aimed at universality and orthodoxy. "My system, if I may venture to give it so fine a name, is the only attempt I know ever made to reduce all knowledges into harmony. It opposes no other system, but shows what was true in each; and how that which was true in the particular, in each of them became error, *because* it was only half the truth. I have endeavored to unite the insulated fragments of truth, and therewith to frame a perfect mirror. I show to each system that I fully understand and rightly appreciate what that system means; but then I lift up that system to a higher point of view, from which I enable it to see its former position, where it was, indeed, but under another light and with different relations;—so that the fragment of truth is not only acknowledged, but explained" (*Table Talk,* Sept. 12, 1831, in W. G. T. Shedd, ed., *The Complete Works of Samuel Taylor Coleridge* [7 vols.; New York, Harper, 1854], VI, 373–374).

[2] "The distinction of Coleridge, which puts him head and shoulders above every other English critic, is due to his introduction of a philosophical method of criticism" (Sir Herbert Read, "Coleridge as Critic," in *Lectures in Criticism,* ed. R. P. Blackmur [New York, Pantheon Books, 1949], p. 88).

[3] Cf. D. G. James, *Skepticism and Poetry* (London, Allen and Unwin, 1937).

[4] Coleridge's position prohibits him from attempting a literally complete classification of genres, which would be a lifeless product of the understanding. ("Aristotle was, and still is, the sovereign lord of the understanding;—the faculty judging by the senses. He was a conceptualist, and never could raise himself into that higher state which was natural to Plato, and has been so to others, in which the understanding is distinctly contemplated, and, as it were, looked down upon from the throne of actual ideas, or living, inborn, essential truths" [July 2, 1830, *Table Talk*]. Coleridge, that is, accepted and used the Aristotelian classification, but was interested in genre primarily as an idea.)

[5] "Balance" is always for Coleridge one aspect of the reconciliation of opposites.

[6] Without attempting exhaustive accuracy, I have counted thirteen significant instances of the use of these terms in *Collected Letters of Samuel Taylor Coleridge,* ed. E. L. Griggs (4 vols.; Oxford, Clarendon Press, 1956——), Vols. I, II; eight in *Coleridge's Miscellaneous Criticism,* ed. T. M. Raysor (Cambridge, Harvard University Press, 1936); eight in *Biographia Literaria;* seven in *Coleridge's Shakespearean Criticism,* ed. T. M. Raysor (2 vols.; Cambridge, Harvard University Press, 1930); and six in *Table Talk.*

[7] *Coleridge's Shakespearean Criticism,* I, 196.

[8] That is, it is possible to have an *idea* of the class "swan," but not a *conception* of "bird-beauty." "By an idea I mean . . . that conception of a thing, which is not abstracted from any particular state, form, or mode, in which the thing may happen to exist at this or that time; nor yet generalized from any number or succession of such forms or modes; but which is given by the knowledge of its ultimate

aim. . . . A conception, consists in a conscious act of the understanding, bringing any given object or impression into the same class with any number of other objects or impressions by means of some character or characters common to them all" (*On the Constitution of the Church and State,* in Shedd, *op. cit.*, VI, 30–31).

[9] "[The most general law of life is] polarity, or the essential dualism of Nature, arising out of its productive unity, and still tending to reaffirm it, either as equilibrium, indifference, or identity" (Appendix C, *Aids to Reflection,* in Shedd, *op. cit.*, I, 391).

[10] ". . . that the one in order to its manifestation must appear in and as two . . ." ("Notes on Jeremy Taylor," in Shedd, *op. cit.*, V, 219). ". . . this anti-monadic feeling, this (what shall I say?) *knowing, feeling,* a man to be *one,* yet not understanding how to think of him but as two . . ." (*Inquiring Spirit,* ed. Kathleen Coburn [New York, Pantheon Books, 1951], p. 31).

[11] "There are two principles in every European and Christian state: Permanency and Progression. In the civil wars of the seventeenth century in England, which are as new and fresh now as they were a hundred and sixty years ago, and will be so forever to us, these two principles came to a struggle" (Jan. 1, 1823, *Table Talk,* p. 259). See also *On the Constitution of the Church and State,* pp. 38–39. Upon the question of the reconciliation of opposites the following statement is representative of many: "Let me call attention to the essential difference between 'opposite' and 'contrary.' Opposite powers are always of the same kind, and tend to union, either by equipoise or by a common product. Thus the + and − poles of the magnet, thus positive and negative electricity, are opposites. Sweet and sour are opposites; sweet and bitter are contraries. The feminine character is opposed to the masculine; but the effeminate is its contrary. Even so in the present instance, the interest of permanence is opposed to that of progressiveness; but so far from being contrary interests, they, like the magnetic forces, suppose and require each other. Even the most mobile of creatures, the serpent, makes a rest of its own body, and, drawing up its voluminous train from behind, on this *fulcrum* propels itself onward" (*On the Constitution of the Church and State,* p. 38n.). See also *Biographia Literaria,* ed. John Shawcross (2 vols.; Oxford, Clarendon Press, 1907), I, 85–86; "In every voluntary movement we first counteract gravitation, in order to avail ourselves of it. It must exist, that there may be a something to be counteracted, and which, by its re-action, may aid the force that is exerted to resist it. Let us consider what we do when we leap. We first resist the gravitating power by an act purely voluntary, and then by another act, voluntary in part, we yield to it in order to light on the spot, which we had previously proposed to ourselves. . . . Most of my readers will have observed a small water-insect on the surface of rivulets, which throws a cinque-spotted shadow fringed with prismatic colours on the sunny bottom of the brook; and will have noticed, how the little animal *wins* its way up against the stream, by alternate pulses of active and passive motion, now resisting the current, and now yielding to it in order to gather strength and a momentary *fulcrum* for a further propulsion."

[12] *Biographia Literaria,* I, 86.

[13] "The understanding suggests the materials of reasoning: the reason decides upon them. The first can only say, This *is*, or *ought* to be so. The last says, It *must* be so" (Jan. 6, 1823, *Table Talk*, p. 265).

[14] From "Dejection: An Ode."

[15] *Biographia Literaria*, I, 202.

[16] *Ibid.*, II, 8.

[17] *Coleridge's Miscellaneous Criticism*, p. 102. "Rabelais is a most wonderful writer. Pantagruel is the Reason; Panurge the Understanding,—the pollarded man, the man with every faculty except the reason" (June 15, 1830, *Table Talk*, p. 333). "Genius of the highest kind implies an unusual intensity of the modifying power, which, detached from the discriminative and reproductive power, might conjure a platted straw into a royal diadem . . ." (May 1, 1833, *ibid.*, p. 446). "Genius must have talent as its complement and implement, just as, in like manner, imagination must have fancy. In short, the higher intellectual powers can only act through a corresponding energy of the lower" (Aug. 20, 1833, *ibid.*, p. 481).

[18] *Biographia Literaria*, II, 12.

[19] "As according to an old saying, 'an ill foreknown is half disarmed,' I will here notice an inconvenience in our language, which, without a greater inconvenience, I could not avoid, in the use of the term 'State' in a double sense; a larger, in which it is equivalent to realm and includes the Church, and a narrower, in which it is distinguished *quasi per antithesin* from the Church, as in the phrase, Church and State. But the context, I trust, will in every instance prevent ambiguity" (*On the Constitution of the Church and State*, p. 37). This usage, despite Coleridge's apology for it here, is inherent in his method of thought and deeply significant. As noticed above, the first term in Coleridge's antitheses is usually double, with a "narrower" and a "larger" sense; narrowly it is a part of the antithesis, but more broadly it is also the *tertium quid* or product of the antithesis reconciled. Thus the pairing in Coleridge's vocabulary of Reason-Understanding, Idea-Conception, Imagination-Fancy, Imitation-Copy, Genius-Talent, Organic-Mechanical, Principle-Rule, Romantic-Classical, and Humor-Wit. See above, nn. 1, 4.

[20] *Biographia Literaria*, II, 12.

[21] *Ibid.*, I, 202.

[22] *Ibid.*, I, 86.

[23] "Coleridge's theories of imagination and organic unity were developed together, and complement each other. Their relation is that of subject to object, as Coleridge might say. Organic unity is his name for the imaginative totality of a poem, which lends aesthetic integration and symbolic meaning to the words and images, stanzas or scenes, that constitute its parts. One's interpretation of the meaning of organic unity is necessarily determined by one's conception of the Coleridgean imagination. In the light of a psychological interpretation of imagination, the unity with which this mental power informs its works is explicable in psychological and literary terms, and is related to the organic life of nature by analogy only, or by way of the human mind. If one remembers that the word 'organic' is used figuratively, its connotations need not be misleading" (Kenneth Millar, "The In-

ward Eye" [unpublished Ph.D. dissertation, University of Michigan, 1951], p. 386).

[24] For the fullest account of the "living plant" analogy see Meyer H. Abrams, *The Mirror and the Lamp* (New York, Oxford University Press, 1953), esp. pp. 169–175.

[25] *Coleridge's Shakespearean Criticism,* I, 224.

[26] This corresponds with the role of imagination as mediator between the reason and the understanding. "One diagnostic or contra-distinguishing mark appertaining to all ideas is, that they are not adequately expressible by words. An idea can only be expressed (more correctly suggested) by two contradictory positions; as, for example: the soul is all in every part;—nature is a sphere, the centre of which is everywhere, and its circumference nowhere, and the like" ("Notes on Jeremy Taylor," pp. 206–207).

[27] "No simile runs on all four legs (*nihil simile est idem*) . . ." (*On the Constitution of the Church and State,* p. 79). See also *Biographia Literaria,* II, 112–113.

[28] *Biographia Literaria,* I, 44.

[29] "I saw that the excellence of this kind consisted in just and acute observations on men and manners in an artificial state of society, as its matter and substance: and in the logic of wit, conveyed in smooth and strong epigrammatic couplets, as its *form.* Even when the subject was addressed to the fancy, or the intellect, as in the Rape of the Lock, or the Essay on Man; nay, when it was a consecutive narration, as in that astonishing product of matchless talent and ingenuity, Pope's Translation of the Iliad; still a point was looked for at the end of each second line, and the whole was as it were a sorites, or, if I may exchange a logical for a grammatical metaphor, a *conjunction disjunctive,* of epigrams" (*ibid.,* I, 11). "Dr. Johnson seems to have been really more powerful in discoursing *viva voce* in conversation than with his pen in his hand. It seems as if the excitement of company called something like reality and consecutiveness into his reasonings, which in his writings I can not see" (Nov. 1, 1833, *Table Talk,* p. 495).

[30] See *Coleridge's Shakespearean Criticism,* I, 219 f.

[31] *Ibid.,* I, 37.

[32] *Ibid.*

[33] *Coleridge's Miscellaneous Criticism,* pp. 341–342.

[34] *Coleridge's Shakespearean Criticism,* I, 5 f.

[35] *Ibid.,* I, 131 f.

[36] *Ibid.,* I, 18.

[37] *Ibid.,* I, 4–5.

[38] *Ibid.,* I, 6.

[39] *Ibid.,* I, 20.

[40] *Ibid.,* I, 36.

[41] *Ibid.*

## CHAPTER 2.

[1] For commentary see John H. Muirhead, *Coleridge as Philosopher* (New York, Macmillan, 1930), pp. 127–136; and Alice D. Snyder,

*Coleridge on Logic and Learning* (New Haven, Yale University Press, 1929), pp. 16–23.

[2] Snyder, *op. cit.*, discusses its relations to contemporary scientific and medical controversies.

[3] "In the language of the old Schools, Unity + Omnity = Totality" (Appendix B, *The Statesman's Manual*, in W. G. T. Shedd, ed., *The Complete Works of Samuel Taylor Coleridge* [7 vols.; New York, Harper, 1854], I, 456). Note also a recently published annotation by Coleridge of the 1812 edition of *The Friend:* "Life can be defined only by Individuation / that which manifests it's individuality is Life to *us*,—that, which existing, as a whole, contains in itself the principle of the specific form, by which it manifests itself as a whole" (Jonathan Wordsworth, "Some Unpublished Coleridge Marginalia," *TLS*, June 14, 1957, p. 369).

[4] Cf. Gordon McKenzie, *Organic Unity in Coleridge* (Berkeley, University of California Press, 1939), contra. For Mr. McKenzie organic unity develops and diverges from the triadic system of reconciling opposites in not demanding strict logical oppositions, but admitting mere discords as well. Organic unity is less rigid, he considers, than the reconciliation of opposites, and "may be used to describe the work of art in a more illuminating way because it agrees more closely with human experience" (pp. 35–36). But see René Wellek, "Coleridge's Philosophy and Criticism," in *The English Romantic Poets*, ed. T. M. Raysor (rev. ed.; New York, Modern Language Association of America, 1956), pp. 130–131: "But mistakenly, I think, too sharp a distinction is drawn between the principle of the reconciliation of opposites and the principle of organc unity. . . . The dialectical reconciliation of opposites is a development of the organic principles . . . and not the other way round."

[5] *Theory of Life*, in Shedd, *op. cit.*, I, 387.

[6] *Ibid.*, p. 388.

[7] *Ibid.*, pp. 389–390.

[8] *Ibid.*, pp. 391–392.

[9] *Ibid.*, p. 399.

[10] *Ibid.*, p. 397.

[11] For Coleridge the relationship is symbolic rather than analogical, because the connections are *real;* a symbol is "a sign included in the idea which it represents;—that is, an actual part chosen to represent the whole, as a lip with a chin prominent is a symbol of man; or a lower form or *species* of a higher in the same kind; thus magnetism is the symbol of vegetation, and of the vegetative and reproductive power in animals; the instinct of the ant-tribe or the bee is a symbol of the human understanding" (*Aids to Reflection*, in Shedd, *op. cit.*, I, 270n.).

[12] *Theory of Life*, p. 399. Coleridge's insistence upon the symbolic rather than analogical relationship should be borne in mind against the view of M. H. Abrams, expressed in his important study of romantic criticism, that Coleridge's consistency "is not primarily logical, or even psychological, but analogical" (*The Mirror and the Lamp* [New York, Oxford University Press, 1953], p. 170).

[13] *Theory of Life*, p. 401.

[14] *Ibid.*

[15] *Ibid.*, p. 403. "Wonderful are the efforts of Nature to reconcile chasm with continuity, to vault and nevertheless to glide, though in truth the continuity alone belongs to Nature, the chasms are the effect of a higher principle, limiting the duration and regulating the retention of the products. From the Vermes to the Mammalia, Organic Nature is in every class and everywhere tending to individuality . . ." (manuscript quoted from Muirhead, *op. cit.*, p. 121).

[16] *Theory of Life*, p. 412.

[17] Cf. Muirhead, *op. cit.*, pp. 135–136; Abrams, *op. cit.*, pp. 220–221. Abrams calls the *Theory of Life* "Coleridge's organismic version of the Great Chain of Being," and remarks that it "is obvious that this scale of nature may readily be generalized into a comprehensive standard of value, ethical and aesthetic."

[18] "For as to abstract the idea of *kind* from that of *degrees*, which are alone designated in the language of common use, is the first and indispensable step in philosophy, so are we the better enabled to form a notion of the *kind*, the lower the *degree* and the simpler the form is in which it appears to us. We study the complex in the simple; and only from the intuition of the lower can we safely proceed to the intellection of the higher degrees. The only danger lies in the leaping from low to high, with the neglect of the intervening gradations. . . . That these degrees will themselves bring forth secondary kinds sufficiently distinct for all the purposes of science, and even for common sense, will be seen in the course of this inquisition: for this is one proof of the essential vitality of nature, that she does not ascend as links in a suspended chain, but as the steps in a ladder; or rather she at one and the same time *ascends* as by a climax, and expands as the concentric circles on the lake from the point to which the stone in its fall had given the first impulse" (*Theory of Life*, p. 386).

[19] *Ibid.*, pp. 390, 416.

[20] *Ibid.*, p. 390.

[21] *Collected Letters of Samuel Taylor Coleridge*, ed. E. L. Griggs (4 vols.; Oxford, Clarendon Press, 1956——), II, 1196–1197.

[22] *Ibid.*, II, 1193.

[23] "What those vital forces that seem to bear an analogy to the imponderable agents, magnetic, or galvanic, in bodies inorganic, if indeed they are not the same in a higher energy and under a different law of action—what these, I say, are in the living body in distinction from the fluids in the glands and vessels—the same or at least holding a like relation, are the indeterminable, but yet actual, influences of intellect, information, prevailing principles and tendencies . . . to the regular, definite, and legally recognized powers in the body politic" (*On the Constitution of the Church and State*, in Shedd, *op. cit.*, VI, 78–79; see pp. 65, 69, and 72 for other references to the term "body politic").

[24] "I am aware of few subjects more calculated to awake a deep at once practical and speculative interest in a philosophic mind than the analogies between organic (I might say, organific) Life and Will. The Facts both of Physiology and Pathology lead to one and the same conclusion—viz.—that in some way or other the Will is the obscure

*Radical* of the Vital Power" (*Unpublished Letters of Samuel Taylor Coleridge,* ed. E. L. Griggs [2 vols.; New Haven, Yale University Press, 1933], II, 335).

[25] "The sun calls up the vapour—attenuates, lifts it—it becomes a cloud—and now it is the Veil of the Divinity—the Divinity transpiercing it at once hides and declares his presence. We *see,* we are conscious of *Light* alone, but it is Light embodied in the earthly nature, which that Light itself awoke and sublimated. What is the Body, but the fixture of the mind? the stereotype Impression?" (*Ibid.,* II, 46–47.)

[26] "The primary IMAGINATION I hold to be the living Power and prime Agent of all human Perception, and as a repetition in the finite mind of the eternal act of creation in the infinite I AM" (*Biographia Literaria,* ed. John Shawcross [2 vols.; Oxford, Clarendon Press, 1907], I, 202).

[27] "For the property of passion is not to *create;* but to set in increased activity" (*ibid.,* II, 42).

[28] "The common end of all *narrative,* nay, of *all,* Poems is to convert a *series* into a *Whole:* to make those events, which in real or imagined History move on in a *strait* Line, assume to our Understandings a *circular* motion—the snake with it's Tail in it's mouth" (*Unpublished Letters,* II, 128).

[29] "Nothing *sets off* a thing better, than a sharp contrast . . ." (*ibid.,* II, 451).

## Chapter 3.

[1] *Biographia Literaria,* ed. John Shawcross (2 vols.; Oxford, Clarendon Press, 1907), II, 305.

[2] *Ibid.,* II, 221.

[3] *Ibid.,* II, 223.

[4] *Ibid.*

[5] *Ibid.,* II, 225.

[6] *Ibid.,* II, 226–227.

[7] *Ibid.,* II, 235–236.

[8] *Ibid.,* II, 227. The imagination is "that reconciling and mediatory power, which incorporating the reason in images of the sense, and organizing (as it were) the flux of the senses by the permanence and self-circling energies of the reason, gives birth to a system of symbols . . ." (*The Statesman's Manual,* in W. G. T. Shedd, ed., *The Complete Works of Samuel Taylor Coleridge* [7 vols.; New York, Harper, 1854], I, 436).

[9] *Biographia Literaria,* II, 247.

[10] *Ibid.,* II, 248.

[11] *Ibid.,* II, 243.

[12] *Ibid.,* II, 231.

[13] *Ibid.,* II, 233.

[14] *Ibid.,* II, 243.

[15] *Ibid.,* II, 248.

[16] *Ibid.,* II, 253.

[17] *Ibid.,* II, 254.

[18] *Ibid.*, II, 259.
[19] *Ibid.*, II, 256.
[20] *Ibid.*, II, 257.
[21] *Ibid.*, II, 232.
[22] *Ibid.*, II, 230.
[23] *Ibid.*, II, 232.
[24] Individuation is "the power which unites a given *all* into a *whole* that is presupposed by all its parts," and in its highest degree "the unity will be more intense in proportion as it constitutes each particular thing a whole of itself; and yet more, again, in proportion to the number and interdependence of the parts, which it unites as a whole."
[25] *Ibid.*, II, 233.
[26] *Ibid.*, II, 234.
[27] *Ibid.*
[28] *Ibid.*, II, 235. Cf. pp. 250–251: "I am now using beauty in its most comprehensive sense, as including expression and artistic interest,—that is, I consider not only the living balance, but likewise all the accompaniments that even by disturbing are necessary to the renewal and continuance of the balance. And in this sense I proceed to show, that the beautiful in the object may be referred to two elements,—lines and colors; the first belonging to the shapely . . . and in this to the law, and the reason; and the second to the lively, the free, the spontaneous, and the self-justifying."
[29] *Ibid.*, II, 237.
[30] *Ibid.*, II, 238.
[31] *Ibid.*, II, 239.
[32] *Ibid.*
[33] *Ibid.*, II, 244.
[34] *Ibid.*, II, 245.
[35] *Ibid.*, II, 257.
[36] *Ibid.*
[37] *Ibid.*, II, 257–258.
[38] *Ibid.*, II, 258. On the role of the unconscious in Coleridge's literary theory see James V. Baker, *The Sacred River* (Baton Rouge, Louisiana State University Press, 1957).
[39] *Biographia Literaria*, II, 234.
[40] *Ibid.*, II, 260.
[41] *Ibid.*, II, 239.
[42] *Ibid.*, II, 263–264.
[43] *Ibid.*, II, 263.
[44] "At its 'apex' nature is essential spirit which is above strictly human terms . . ." (Walter Jackson Bate, "Coleridge on the Function of Art," in *Perspectives of Criticism*, ed. Harry Levin [Cambridge, Harvard University Press, 1950], p. 128).
[45] *Biographia Literaria*, II, 254–255.
[46] *Ibid.*, II, 257–258.
[47] *Ibid.*, II, 238.

## Chapter 4.

[1] In its root sense, ". . . all objects of mere desire constitute an interest (i.e. *aliquid quod est inter hoc et aliud,* or that which is between the agent and his motive), and which is therefore valued only as the means to the end" (*Biographia Literaria,* ed. John Shawcross [2 vols.; Oxford, Clarendon Press, 1907], II, 224).

[2] *Ibid.*, II, 243.

[3] *Ibid.*, II, 259.

[4] *Ibid.*, II, 262.

[5] *Ibid.*, II, 10.

[6] *Ibid.*, II, 220.

[7] *Ibid.*, II, 221.

[8] *Ibid.*, II, 232.

[9] *Ibid.*, II, 11.

[10] *Ibid.*, II, 235. Cf. the "small water-insect" who "*wins* its way up against the stream, by alternate pulses of active and passive motion. . . . This is no unapt emblem of the mind's self-experience in the act of thinking" (*ibid.*, I, 85–86). The comparison reveals a common organic unity and ideal movement in the mind and in the aesthetic object.

[11] *Ibid.*, II, 239, 243.

[12] *S. T. Coleridge's Treatise on Method,* ed. Alice D. Snyder (London, Constable, 1934), pp. 62–63.

[13] *Biographia Literaria,* I, 86.

[14] *Ibid.*, I, 202.

[15] *Ibid.*, II, 12.

[16] *Ibid.*, II, 227.

[17] *Ibid.*, I, 178.

[18] *Ibid.*, I, 202.

[19] *Ibid.*, I, 272.

[20] Walter Jackson Bate, "Coleridge on the Function of Art," in *Perspectives of Criticism,* ed. Harry Levin (Cambridge, Harvard University Press, 1950), pp. 145–146. In agreement with Shawcross are D. G. James (*Skepticism and Poetry* [London, Allen and Unwin, 1937], pp. 15–18); and Basil Willey, *Nineteenth Century Studies: Coleridge to Matthew Arnold* (New York, Oxford University Press, 1949), pp. 13–14. Willey writes, "This is not to be dismissed as metaphysical babble; a weight of thought, indeed a whole philosophy, lies beneath each phrase. . . . In speaking thus of the Primary Imagination, then, Coleridge is affirming that the mind is essentially and inveterately creative: 'we receive but what we give,' and in the commonest everyday acts of perception we are making our own world."

[21] *Biographia Literaria,* I, 86.

[22] *Ibid.*, I, 179.

[23] *The Mirror and the Lamp* (New York, Oxford University Press, 1953), p. 68. Abrams' view has much authority behind it, including I. A. Richards, *Coleridge on Imagination* (New York, W. W. Norton, 1950), pp. 157–163; and Willey, *op. cit.*, p. 15.

[24] *Biographia Literaria,* II, 11.

[25] See Richards, *op. cit.*, p. 115: "What he did was to introduce one of the finest red-herrings in all the literature of criticism."

[26] According to the report of J. Tomalin, Coleridge offered this alternative explanation in the third of his 1811–12 lectures: "So closely connected, he continued, was metre with passion that many of the finest passages we read in prose are in themselves, in point of metre, poetry—only they are forms of metre which we have not been familiarized to and [are] not brought forward to us and other English readers in the shape of metre. Coleridge had paid particular attention to the language of the Bible and had found that all persons had been affected with a sense of their high poetic character, not merely from the thoughts conveyed in them, but from the language enclosing those thoughts—from the stately march of the words, which had affected them in a degree and kind altogether different from that of common writing, and different from the narrative and preceptive parts of the same books. It had been his business to discover the cause, and he had found that in almost every passage brought before him, as having produced a particular effect, there was metre and very often poetry" (*Coleridge's Shakespearean Criticism*, ed. T. M. Raysor [2 vols.; Cambridge, Harvard University Press, 1930], II, 79–80). This explanation is on the surface but not, I think, fundamentally incompatible with that furnished in the *Biographia Literaria*.

[27] *Biographia Literaria*, II, 262.

[28] *Ibid.*, II, 238.

[29] "The theory of poetry set forth in the *Biographia Literaria* forms a coherent whole, but it is too good a theory for all its limitations, to permit of reduction to a single principle or cause. For this reason various modern commentators, including I. A. Richards and Allen Tate, have naturally discovered that Coleridge, great as he was, had only a confused glimpse of the simple truth about his subject. The confusion, however, appears less glaring on a close reading of the text of the *Biographia* than in the pages of these recent interpreters; and much of the trouble disappears when it is observed that Coleridge had not one source for the distinctions he employs but several sources, which are nevertheless correlated in a scheme that allows him to discriminate aspects of poems as determined now by their medium or manner, now by their substance, now by their origin in the mental powers of the poet, now by their immediate or remote ends" (R. S. Crane, "The Critical Monism of Cleanth Brooks," in *Critics and Criticism*, ed. R. S. Crane [Chicago, University of Chicago Press, 1952], p. 86). Mr. Crane is not in sympathy with Coleridge's doctrine of organic unity, but his analysis of Coleridge's critical distinctions in the essay quoted is acute beyond precedent.

[30] *Biographia Literaria*, II, 12.

[31] "When Coleridge talked in terms of the distinction between the reason and the understanding he was, of course, accepting a 'faculty psychology' that actually belied his own conception of the organic unity of living processes" (Alice D. Snyder, *Coleridge on Logic and Learning* [New Haven, Yale University Press, 1929], p. 15). This charge may also be advanced against the definition of imagination;

but it has been argued here on all occasions that Coleridge reconciles partness with wholeness.

[32] *Coleridge's Shakespearean Criticism,* I, 163–164.

[33] *Biographia Literaria,* II, 14–19. Cf. I, 64: "My friend [Wordsworth] has drawn a masterly sketch of the branches with their poetic fruitage. I wish to add the trunk, and even the roots as far as they lift themselves above ground, and are visible to the naked eye of our common consciousness." Poetry is simple, sensuous, and passionate. The simplicity of poetry "supposes a smooth and finished road, on which the reader is to walk onward easily, with streams murmuring by his side, and trees and flowers and human dwellings to make his journey as delightful as the object of it is desirable . . ." (*Coleridge's Shakespearean Criticism,* I, 165).

[34] *Biographia Literaria,* II, 49–50.

[35] *Ibid.,* II, 56.

[36] *Ibid.,* II, 64.

[37] See Abrams, *op. cit.,* pp. 173–175, 223–225.

[38] E.g., by Sir Herbert Read, "Coleridge as Critic," in *Lectures in Criticism,* ed. R. P. Blackmur (New York, Pantheon Books, 1949).

[39] *Biographia Literaria,* I, 19.

[40] *Biographia Literaria,* II, 258.

[41] See Walter Jackson Bate, *From Classicism to Romanticism* (Cambridge, Harvard University Press, 1946), p. 184.

## Chapter 5.

[1] Cf. *Biographia Literaria,* ed. John Shawcross (2 vols.; Oxford, Clarendon Press, 1907), II, 33n.

[2] *Ibid.,* II, 63. For Coleridge a principle, like an idea, is always vital. Edmund Burke "referred habitually to *principles.* He was a *scientific* statesman; and therefore a *seer.* For every principle contains in itself the germs of a prophecy" (*ibid.,* I, 125).

[3] *Ibid.,* II, 85. Cf. II, 14–15, 44, 65.

[4] *Ibid.,* II, 33–34. Cf. II, 101.

[5] Coleridge goes on to explain that his reconciliation is identical with "individuation," though he does not use the term in the passage itself: "Say not that I am recommending abstractions; for these class-characteristics which constitute the instructiveness of a character, are so modified and particularized in each person of the Shakespearean Drama, that life itself does not excite more distinctly that sense of individuality which belongs to real existence" (*ibid.,* II, 33n.). Some pages later, in commenting upon the words *essential* and *essence,* he defines essence as "the principle of *individuation,* the inmost principle of the possibility of any thing, as that particular thing" (*ibid.,* II, 47).

[6] *Ibid.,* II, 34–36.

[7] *Collected Letters of Samuel Taylor Coleridge,* ed. E. L. Griggs (4 vols.; Oxford, Clarendon Press, 1956——), I, 334 (hereafter to be cited as *Collected Letters*). David V. Erdman finds a resemblance between Coleridge's conception of Wordsworth and his portrait of George Washington in a group of *Morning Post* essays ("Coleridge

on George Washington: Newly Discovered Essays of 1800," *Bulletin of the New York Public Library,* LXI [1957], 81–97).

[8] *Collected Letters,* I, 391.

[9] *Ibid.,* I, 491.

[10] *Ibid.,* I, 582.

[11] *Ibid.,* I, 584. See also I, 658; II, 714.

[12] See "To William Wordsworth," ll. 49–54:

> With stedfast eye I viewed thee in the choir
> Of ever-enduring men. The truly great
> Have all one age, and from one visible space
> Shed influence! They, both in power and act,
> Are permanent, and Time is not with them,
> Save as it worketh for them, they in it.

T. S. Eliot's "Tradition and the Individual Talent," with its reconciliation of history and criticism in the temporal and the timeless, forms an interesting parallel to Coleridge. See *Selected Essays of T. S. Eliot* (New York, Harcourt, Brace, 1950), pp. 4–5.

[13] The fullest and most reliable contemporary account of the relationship is contained in *Henry Crabb Robinson on Books and Their Writers,* ed. Edith J. Morley (3 vols.; London, J. M. Dent and Sons, 1938).

[14] Cf. Wordsworth, 1800 Preface to the *Lyrical Ballads:* "For all good poetry is the spontaneous overflow of powerful feelings: and though this be true, Poems to which any value can be attached were never produced on any variety of subjects but by a man who, being possessed of more than usual organic sensibility, had also thought long and deeply."

[15] See *Biographia Literaria,* I, 56–60. George Whalley argues that Coleridge's exposition of Wordsworth's poetry is the unifying principle of the *Biographia* ("The Integrity of *Biographia Literaria,*" in *Essays and Studies Collected for the English Association,* n.s., VI [London, 1953]).

[16] *Collected Letters,* II, 1033–1034.

[17] "The approbation he [Wordsworth] has met with from *some* superior persons compensates for the loss of popularity, though no man has completely understood him—Coleridge not excepted, who is not happy enough to enter into his feelings. 'I am myself,' said he, 'one of the happiest of men . . .'" (Morley, *op. cit.,* I, 73).

[18] "The poet, described in *ideal* perfection, brings the whole soul of man into activity, with the subordination of its faculties to each other, according to their relative worth and dignity" (*Biographia Literaria,* II, 12).

[19] *Ibid.,* II, 95.

[20] *Ibid.,* II, 71–73.

[21] *Ibid.,* II, 77.

[22] *Ibid.,* II, 78.

[23] *Ibid.,* II, 96.

[24] *Ibid.,* II, 84.

[25] *Ibid.,* II, 129.

[26] *Ibid.,* II, 95.

[27] *Ibid.,* II, 97.

[28] *Ibid.*
[29] *Ibid.*, II, 50.
[30] *Ibid.*, II, 11.
[31] *Ibid.*, II, 98.
[32] Cf. *Theory of Life,* in W. G. T. Shedd, *The Complete Works of Samuel Taylor Coleridge* (7 vols.; New York, Harper, 1854), Vol. I.
[33] *Biographia Literaria,* II, 101.
[34] *Ibid.*, II, 64.
[35] *Ibid.*, II, 102–103.
[36] Cf. *ibid.*, II, 16–18, on the proofs of original genius in poetic imagery; and I. A. Richards' commentary in *Coleridge on Imagination* (New York, W. W. Norton, 1950), pp. 82–84. See also *Collected Letters,* I, 349, 511 ("I could half suspect that what are deemed fine descriptions, produce their effects almost purely by a charm of words, with which & with whose combinations, we associate *feelings* indeed, but no distinct *Images*").
[37] *Biographia Literaria,* II, 102–103.
[38] *Ibid.*, II, 104. The passage suggests the social and political implications that Wordsworth, Shelley, and Coleridge himself found in the romantic "sympathetic imagination."
[39] *Ibid.*, II, 6. Coleridge might have remembered his own errors, as in his early lines "To a Young Ass":

> Innocent foal! thou poor despis'd forlorn!
> I hail thee *Brother*—spite of the fool's scorn!

[40] *Ibid.*, II, 107.
[41] *Ibid.*, II, 109.
[42] *Ibid.*, II, 9.
[43] *Ibid.*, II, 109.
[44] *Ibid.*, II, 13.
[45] *Ibid.*, II, 110.
[46] See Frederick A. Pottle, "The Eye and the Object in the Poetry of Wordsworth," in *Wordsworth Centenary Studies,* ed. G. T. Dunklin (Princeton, Princeton University Press, 1951), for an account of "The Daffodils" in Wordsworth's own terms.
[47] *Biographia Literaria,* II, 113.
[48] See the defense of these lines in Cleanth Brooks, "Wordsworth and the Paradox of the Imagination," in *The Well Wrought Urn* (New York, Reynal and Hitchcock, 1947), pp. 122–123, 129–137.
[49] *Biographia Literaria,* II, 114.
[50] *Ibid.*, I, 4.
[51] *Ibid.*, I, 12.
[52] *Ibid.*, II, 114–115. See also *Coleridge's Shakespearean Criticism,* ed. T. M. Raysor (2 vols.; Cambridge, Harvard University Press, 1930), I, 166: "The second condition, sensuousness, insures that framework of objectivity, that definiteness and articulation of imagery, and that modification of the images themselves, without which poetry becomes flattened into mere didactics of practice or evaporated into a hazy, unthoughtful, day-dreaming; and the third condition, passion, provides that neither thought nor imagery shall be simply objective, but that the *passio vera* of humanity shall warm and animate both."
[53] *Biographia Literaria,* II, 115.

[54] Cf. *ibid.*, I, 14–15.

[55] *Ibid.*, II, 115–116. Cf. I. A. Richards on sense, feeling, tone, and intention, in his *Practical Criticism* (London, Routledge and Kegan Paul, 1929), p. 181 f.

[56] *Biographia Literaria*, II, 117.

[57] *Ibid.*, II, 5; cf. II, 64.

[58] *Ibid.*, I, 59.

[59] Cf. *ibid.*, I, 163–167.

[60] *Ibid.*, II, 120.

[61] See *ibid.*, I, 86, 202; *Coleridge's Shakespearean Criticism*, I, 198; and above, p. 63.

[62] *Biographia Literaria*, II, 121.

[63] *Ibid.*, II, 102; cf. II, 16.

[64] On this frequently used term of Coleridge's critical vocabulary see J. Isaacs, "Coleridge's Critical Terminology," in *Essays and Studies by Members of the English Association*, XXI (1935), 101. Mr. Isaacs justly relates *genial* to *genius* ("pertaining to genius"), but one suspects that Coleridge adds its wider, looser, and more generally accepted meaning as well, thus refusing to separate thought and feeling. His critical relations with favored writers are usually affectionate.

[65] *Biographia Literaria*, II, 121.

[66] *Ibid.*, II, 122–123.

[67] *Ibid.*, II, 123.

[68] *Ibid.*, II, 103–109.

[69] *Ibid.*, II, 124. Cf. Morley, *op. cit.*, I, 52: "He [Coleridge] spoke of Calderon, defining him to be a Shakespeare but without his philosophy—having all his imagination and fancy. His usual distinction between these last-mentioned qualities he repeated on this occasion [Nov. 24, 1811], assigning great fancy but no imagination to Southey, and much imagination but a sterile fancy to Wordsworth." Wordsworth made an interesting comparison between Coleridge and himself with respect to the parallel distinction of genius and talent: "His genius he thought great, but his talents he thought still greater & it is in the union of so much genius with so much talent that he thought C. surpassed all other men. W., in a digression, remarked of himself that he had comparatively but little talent: genius was his peculiar faculty" (Henry Crabb Robinson, *Blake, Coleridge, Wordsworth, Lamb, Etc.*, ed. Edith J. Morley [Manchester, at the University Press, 1922], p. 49). One may recall that Coleridge once embroiled himself with Charles Lamb by citing Lamb as an example of talent and himself as an instance of genius.

[70] *Biographia Literaria*, I, 56. Cf. *ibid.*, II, 19, for Shakespeare's early poetry, in which "the creative power and the intellectual energy wrestle as in a war embrace. Each in its excess of strength seems to threaten the extinction of the other."

[71] *Ibid.*, II, 57–58.

[72] *Ibid.*, II, 128. See also *The Notebooks of Samuel Taylor Coleridge, 1794–1804*, ed. Kathleen Coburn (2 vols.; London, Routledge and Kegan Paul, 1957), I (text), 926.

[73] *Biographia Literaria*, II, 129.

[74] *Letters of Samuel Taylor Coleridge*, ed. E. H. Coleridge (2 vols.;

Boston and New York, Houghton, Mifflin, 1895), II, 641–642. See also *Collected Letters*, IV, 564.

[75] Cf. *Biographia Literaria*, II, 33, 101.

[76] *Letters of Samuel Taylor Coleridge*, II, 645–646. See also *Collected Letters*, IV, 572–573.

[77] *Letters of Samuel Taylor Coleridge*, II, 647–648; cf. *Collected Letters*, IV, 574.

[78] *Letters of Samuel Taylor Coleridge*, II, 648; cf. *Collected Letters*, IV, 574.

[79] See Wordsworth's "Tintern Abbey," ll. 102–107:

Therefore am I still
A lover of the meadows and the woods,
And mountains; and of all that we behold
From this green earth; of all the mighty world
Of eye and ear,—both what they half create,
And what perceive . . . ,

and "The Recluse," ll. 811–824:

. . . by words
Which speak of nothing more than what we are
Would I arouse the sensual from their sleep
Of Death, and win the vacant and the vain
To noble raptures; while my voice proclaims
How exquisitely the individual Mind
(And the progressive powers perhaps no less
Of the whole species) to the external World
Is fitted:—and how exquisitely, too—
Theme this but little heard of among men—
The External World is fitted to the Mind;
And the creation (by no lower name
Can it be called) which they with blended might
Accomplish:—this is our high argument.

[80] Cf. the "ascending scale" of the senses in "On the Principles of Genial Criticism," *Biographia Literaria*, II, 237–238.

[81] *Letters of Samuel Taylor Coleridge*, II, 648; cf. *Collected Letters*, IV, 574.

[82] *Letters of Samuel Taylor Coleridge*, II, 648–649; cf. *Collected Letters*, 574–575.

[83] See as an instance "The Pains of Sleep":

Such punishments, I said, were due
To natures deepliest stained with sin,—
For aye entempesting anew
The unfathomable hell within,
The horror of their deeds to view,
To know and loathe, yet wish and do!
Such griefs with such men well agree,
But wherefore, wherefore fall on me? [Ll. 43–50.]

[84] See Wordsworth's "Lines Written in Early Spring":

To her fair works did Nature link
The human soul that through me ran;
And much it grieved my heart to think
What man has made of man.

[85] See below, pp. 135, 150, 152.
[86] *Biographia Literaria,* I, 129.
[87] *Letters of Samuel Taylor Coleridge,* II, 649; cf. *Collected Letters,* IV, 575.
[88] "To William Wordsworth," ll. 2–11.
[89] *Letters of Samuel Taylor Coleridge,* II, 649–650; cf. *Collected Letters,* IV, 575–576.
[90] Among discussions of Coleridge's criticism of Wordsworth the following are especially noteworthy: J. Shawcross in his Supplementary Note, *Biographia Literaria,* I, xcii–xcvi; Thomas S. Raysor, "Coleridge's Criticism of Wordsworth," *Publications of the Modern Language Association,* LIV (1939), 496–510; C. D. Thorpe, "The Imagination: Coleridge versus Wordsworth," *Philological Quarterly,* XVIII (1939), 1–18; T. S. Eliot, "Wordsworth and Coleridge," in *The Use of Poetry and the Use of Criticism* (London, Faber and Faber, 1933); and Earl Leslie Griggs, "Wordsworth through Coleridge's Eyes," in *Wordworth Centenary Studies.* It will be noticed that my own treatment deals with Wordsworth exclusively as a subject for and an occasion of the criticism of Coleridge. S. M. Parrish has recently defended Wordsworth against Coleridge in "The Wordsworth-Coleridge Controversy," *PMLA,* LXIII (1958), 367–374.

## Chapter 6.

[1] "Shakespeare knew the human mind, and its most minute and intimate workings, and he never introduces a word, or a thought, in vain or out of place: if we do not understand him, it is our own fault or the fault of copyists and typographers; but study, and the possession of some small stock of the knowledge by which he worked, will enable us often to detect and explain his meaning. He never wrote at random, or hit upon points of character and conduct by chance; and the smallest fragment of his mind not unfrequently gives a clue to a most perfect, regular, and consistent whole" (*Coleridge's Shakespearean Criticism,* ed. T. M. Raysor [2 vols.; Cambridge, Harvard University Press, 1930], II, 145, reported by John Payne Collier).
[2] In Raysor's two volumes (*op. cit.*) I have counted 234 significant references to the organic method.
[3] ". . . to judge aright, and with the distinct consciousness of the grounds of our judgment, concerning the works of Shakespeare, implies the power and the means of judging rightly of all other works, those of abstract science alone excepted" (Raysor, *op. cit.,* I, 127). ". . . a most profound, energetic, and philosophical mind, without which he might have been a very delightful poet, but not the great dramatic poet . . ." (*ibid.,* I, 214). "He [Shakespeare] is the morning star of philosophy—the guide and pioneer" (*ibid.,* I, 228). "Conceive a profound metaphysician and a great poet, intensely occupied in thinking on all subjects, on the least as well as the greatest—on all the operations of nature and of man, and feeling the importance of all the subjects presented to him—conceive this philosophical part of his character combined with the poetic, the twofold energy constantly acting; the poet and the philosopher embracing, but, as it

were, in a warm embrace, when if both had not been equal, one or the other must have been strangled" (*ibid.*, II, 86–87, reported by J. Tomalin). Cf. *Biographia Literaria*, ed. John Shawcross [2 vols.; Oxford, Clarendon Press, 1907], II, 19; see also Raysor, *op. cit.*, I, 136. There are numerous other such references to Shakespeare.

[4] For "Shakespeare's judgment equal to his genius" see Raysor, *op. cit.*, I, 219–220, 222–224, 228–229; II, 73, 106 f.

[5] *Ibid.*, I, 212–214.

[6] ". . . Shakespeare, himself a nature humanized, a genial understanding directing self-consciously a power and an implicit wisdom deeper than consciousness" (*ibid.*, I, 224). For other references to Shakespeare's godlike power of creation see *ibid.*, I, 85–86, 99, 210, 243, 256; II, 16, 70, 74, 81, 84, 95, 96, 125, 130, 133, 165, 181, 200, 358.

[7] "That such a mind evolved itself in the normal bounds of a human form is a problem indeed" (*ibid.*, I, 244).

[8] See *ibid.*, I, 243–244; II, 70, 74, 115–118, 140, 160–161, 358.

[9] On Coleridge's attitude toward internal evidence see *ibid.*, II, 30, 87, 89, 96, 140–141, 166, 203.

[10] The recurring figure of Proteus, "the one deity of fire and flood," aptly conveys this power of Shakespeare's.

[11] See "Copy" in index to Raysor, *op. cit.*, II, 364.

[12] On the character of the Nurse see *ibid.*, I, 7–8; II, 133–135; for Mistress Quickly, *ibid.*, II, 336, 344.

[13] See *ibid.*, I, 16 (on the character of Brutus), 34, 90, 91, 104.

[14] On the blinding of Gloucester see *ibid.*, I, 66; on the porter scene, I, 75. Other instances are the mourning of the Capulets for the supposedly dead Juliet, I, 11; inconsistency in the character of Gertrude, I, 33; unnaturalness in the messenger who announces Laertes' rebellion, I, 34; anomaly in *Coriolanus* in some speeches by Aufidius, I, 89–91; unnaturalness in Oliver in *As You Like It;* and horror and disgust in *Measure for Measure,* which Coleridge declares to be the only painful part of Shakespeare's genuine works (*ibid.*, I, 113–114).

[15] Coleridge wrote to Davy that in his 1808 lectures he planned to discuss "the genius and writings of Shakespeare, relatively to his predecessors and contemporaries, so as to determine not only his merits and defects, and the proportion that each must bear to the whole, but what of his merits and defects belong to his age, as being found in contemporaries of genius, and what belonged to himself" (*ibid.*, II, 5).

[16] Among references to variety see the discussions of "lyric movements" (*ibid.*, I, 23, 73); of Hamlet's dialogue with the players as "One and among the happiest [instances] of Shakespeare's power of diversifying the scene while he is carrying on the plot" (*ibid.*, I, 30); of the use of relief (*ibid.*, I, 77, 78); and of variety as a quality of romantic drama (*ibid.*, I, 197, 198; "the heterogeneous united as in nature," *ibid.*, I, 228).

[17] *Ibid.*, II, 81.

[18] See *ibid.*, I, 22–23, 78, 80, 96, 149, 150, 153; II, 103, 121–122, 139–140, 184, 191.

[19] See *ibid.*, I, 111, 127–131, 197, 198, 203, 222, 228; II, 120, 169, 212, 247, 248, 357.

[20] "The myriad-minded man, our, and all men's, Shakespeare, has in this piece [*Comedy of Errors*] presented us with a legitimate farce in exactest consonance with the philosophical principles and character of farce, as distinguished from comedy and from entertainments" (*ibid.*, I, 99).

[21] *Ibid.*, I, 126–137; II, 169–181.

[22] Coleridge suggests his conception of this relationship in an early letter to Sir George Beaumont, February 1, 1804. The passage is a significant compendium of the method of his Shakespearean criticism: "Each scene of each play I read, as if it were the whole of Shakespeare's Works—the sole thing extant. I ask myself what are the characteristics—the Diction, the Cadences, and Metre, the character, the passion, the moral or metaphysical Inherences, & fitness for theatric effect, & in what sort of Theatres—all these I write down with great care & precision of Thought & Language—and when I have gone thro' the whole, I shall then collect my papers, & observe, how often such & such Expressions recur & thus shall not only know what the Characteristics of Shakespeare's Plays are, but likewise what proportion they bear to each other" (*Collected Letters of Samuel Taylor Coleridge,* ed. E. L. Griggs [4 vols.; Oxford, Clarendon Press, 1956——], II, 1054). Compare the prospectus for the lecture series of 1818–19: ". . . Mr. Coleridge will give a course of Six Lectures, each having for its subject some one play of Shakespear's, scene by scene, for the purpose of illustrating the conduct of the plot, and the peculiar force, beauty, and propriety, of the language, in the particular passages, as well as the intention of the great Philosophic Poet in the prominent characters of each play, and the unity of interest in the whole and in the apparent contrast of the component parts" (Raysor, *op. cit.*, II, 319).

[23] "This play [*Antony and Cleopatra*] should be perused in mental contrast with Romeo and Juliet; as the love of passion and appetite opposed to the love of affection and instinct" (Raysor, *op. cit.*, I, 86).

[24] See *ibid.*, Vol. I, for references to passion: p. 10, deep passions as atheists, believing in no future; p. 16, the logic of passion; p. 17, the flow of passion; pp. 44–45, in the character of Roderigo; p. 49, the passionless Iago; p. 62, the passions of nature in the storm scenes of *King Lear;* p. 67, the impassioned intellect; p. 86, passion in Cleopatra; p. 109, passion in Cressida; pp. 122–123, the passion of jealousy; p. 149, passion as cause and justification for word plays; p. 159, passion as a justification for breaches of grammar and word order; p. 229, appeals to the passions, not to the appetites; Vol II: p. 74, passion heightened by contrast; pp. 102–104, passion as cause of poetic language; p. 121, passion and the English language; pp. 129, 141–144, the passion of love; p. 130, the passion of pride; pp. 131, 137, the relation of predominant passion to total character; p. 145, the passion of avarice and its absence in Shakespeare's plays; pp. 185–186, the natural and appropriate language of passion. The passages cited reveal, in particular, Coleridge's use of the concept of the ruling

passion, as well as his modifications of it; his consistent relation of passion to figurative language; and the considerations of naturalness, probability, appropriateness, and propriety, which arise from this connection.

[25] See *ibid.*, I, 5, the harmony of a natural landscape; p. 126, "the whole harmonious creation of light and shade"; p. 223, the relation of the bark to the tree; p. 224, organic and mechanic form; p. 242, the poets as plants in soil, or various branches of the same tree; p. 243, Shakespeare a self-sustaining pine; p. 244, his genius a banyan tree; II, 39, a well-tuned instrument of many strings; p. 128, portions and limbs of giant growth; p. 170, the growth of trees and "organic regularity"; pp. 323, 358, the movement of a serpent.

[26] The ideas of motion and progression constantly recur in the Shakespearean criticism. Progression is never linear; it is serpentine, and always reconciled with stillness, as each part is both a step in a movement and an end in itself. "Shakespeare goes on creating, and evolving B. out of A., and C. out of B., and so on, just as a serpent moves, which makes a fulcrum of its own body, and seems for ever twisting and untwisting its own strength" (*Table Talk,* March 5, 1834, reproduced in Raysor, *op. cit.*, II, 358). See also *The Notebooks of Samuel Taylor Coleridge, 1794–1804,* ed. Kathleen Coburn (2 vols.; London, Routledge and Kegan Paul, 1957), I (text), 609.

[27] Coleridge places great stress on Shakespeare's use of anticipation and preparation, because of the importance of beginnings in his scheme of organic growth and relationship. He notes among Shakespeare's characteristics "Expectation in preference to surprize" (Raysor, *op. cit.*, I, 225), along with "Signal adherence to the great law of nature that opposites tend to attract and temper each other." The two observations are akin in the intense and subtle relationship they presuppose as Shakespeare's basic quality. Among discussions of "preparation" see *ibid.*, I, 6, the opening scene of *Romeo and Juliet;* p. 12, the apothecary scene; pp. 20–22, the opening scene of *Hamlet;* p. 22, the preparation for Hamlet by introducing Laertes first; pp. 41–44, first scenes of Shakespeare and the opening of *Hamlet;* pp. 44, 47, 49, preparation in *Othello;* pp. 49, 51, the function of the first act in *Othello;* pp. 55–60, the beginning of *Lear;* p. 63, use of the fool in *Lear;* pp. 67–68, the Weird Sisters in *Macbeth;* and *passim.*

[28] For Shakespeare's use of contrast see *ibid.*, I, 8, 15, 36, 38, 41, 65, 68, 70, 73, 79, 86, 134, 136, 145, 147, 154; II, 73, 104, 134, 177, 194, 207.

[29] See *ibid.*, I, 20, the "gradual rise into tragedy"; p. 21, "exquisitely natural transit into the narration retrospective"; p. 27, the substitution of epic for dramatic diction in the player's speech in Hamlet; p. 40, *idem;* p. 43, gradual transition; p. 67, the bleeding sergeant in *Macbeth;* p. 81, transition in the passions; p. 129, gradation and artistic illusion; p. 156, alternation and transition; p. 205, the infinite gradations between identity and contrariety; II, 111, gradual growth; pp. 144, 156–157, Rosalind-Juliet; pp. 170–171, in the opening of *The Tempest;* p. 174, preparation.

[30] Shift of tempo and change in intensity are discussed most fre-

quently in connection with opening scenes and "lyric movements."

[31] *Germ* and *idea* occur many times in Coleridge's criticism of Shakespeare. It is significant of his fusion of idealism with organicism that they are almost interchangeable.

[32] Raysor, *op. cit.*, I, 5.

[33] "Iago's passionless character, all *will* in intellect" (*ibid.*, I, 49).

[34] *Ibid.*, I, 109–110.

[35] *Ibid.*, I, 9, 12, 54.

[36] This reconciliation is pervasive and omnipresent in Coleridge's criticism, but a few instances of it may be singled out in *ibid.*, Vol. I: p. 9, the treatment of Friar Lawrence; p. 12, "So beautiful as to have been self-justified. Yet what a fine preparation . . ."; pp. 23, 30, relation of plot to scene; p. 130, appropriateness and intrinsic charm; p. 130, reconciliation of means and ends; p. 154, the connection of Shakespeare's characters by likeness and contrast; p. 199, the component arts of the drama; p. 223, "the connection of parts to a whole, so that each part is at once end and means."

[37] Coleridge's constant attention to Shakespeare's meter is itself an evidence of his conception of it as "at once end and means."

[38] "Wherever regular metre can be rendered truly imitative of character, passion, or personal rank, Shakespeare seldom, if ever, neglects it" (Raysor, *op. cit.*, I, 13). See also *ibid.*, pp. 24, 157, 252.

[39] *Ibid.*, I, liv, 206n.

[40] See *ibid.*, I, 4, on unity of interest.

[41] On "dramatic illusion" see *ibid.*, I, 127–131, 199–203; II, 83–87, 321–323; *Biographia Literaria*, II, 157–165, 182–207; *Collected Letters of Samuel Taylor Coleridge*, IV, 641–642; R. H. Fogle, "Coleridge on Dramatic Illusion," *Tulane Drama Review*, IV (1960), 33–44.

[42] Raysor, *op. cit.*, I, 37.

[43] *Ibid.*, I, 204–205. Cf. *Biographia Literaria*, I, 175–186; *Theory of Life*, in W. G. T. Shedd, ed., *The Complete Works of Samuel Taylor Coleridge* (7 vols.; New York, Harper, 1854), I, 390–391, 411–412.

[44] Raysor, *op. cit.*, I, 20–21.

## Chapter 7.

[1] "The antithesis of the beauty of innocence to the beauty of sin" (E. H. Coleridge, ed., *Christabel* [London, Henry Frowde, 1907], p. 15).

[2] Arthur H. Nethercot, *The Road to Tryermaine* (Chicago, University of Chicago Press, 1939), pp. 59–139. See also E. H. Coleridge, *op. cit.*, pp. 6–15.

[3] *Op. cit.*, p. 76.

[4] See E. H. Coleridge, *op. cit.*, pp. 12–15; Nethercot, *op. cit.*, pp. 122–124.

[5] See above, pp. 115–116.

[6] I am forced to disagree with Kathleen Coburn's conclusions in her interesting essay on "Coleridge and Wordsworth and 'the Supernatural,'" *University of Toronto Quarterly*, XXV (1956), 121–130.

Edward E. Bostetter in "Christabel: The Vision of Fear," *Philological Quarterly,* XXXVI (1957), 183–194, emphasizes parallels with Coleridge's own state of mind.

[7] *Op. cit.,* pp. 15–16.

[8] This description might be taxed with inaccuracy in two particulars: that Geraldine looked *askance* at Christabel, and that the look possessed "somewhat of malice, *and more of dread*" (l. 586). It has seemed best nevertheless to let the statement stand as true in context, rather than to modify it. The malice of Geraldine's glance suggests an interesting comparison with Herman Melville's *Billy Budd,* in a scene where the almost sinless Billy is confronted with the depraved Claggart, who is seeking to swear his life away: "Claggart deliberately advanced within short range of Billy, and mesmerically looking him in the eye, briefly recapitulated the accusation.

"Not at first did Billy take it in. When he did the rose-tan of his cheek looked struck as by white leprosy. He stood like one impaled and gagged. Meanwhile the accuser's eyes removing not as yet from the blue dilated ones, underwent a phenomenal change, their wonted rich violet color blurring into a muddy purple. Those lights of human intelligence losing human expression, gelidly protruding like the alien eyes of certain uncatalogued creatures of the deep. The first mesmeric glance was one of surprised fascination; the last was as the hungry lurch of the torpedo-fish."

[9] After this line, the line "Are lean and old and foul of hue" immediately followed in a number of manuscripts.

[10] Cf. ll. 457–459:

> Again she saw that bosom old,
> Again she felt that bosom cold,
> And drew in her breath with a hissing sound.

[11] E. H. Coleridge's account (*op. cit.,* pp. 23–27) of the history of the de Vaux family testifies interestingly to the solidity of the chivalric framework in *Christabel.*

[12] Among discussions of the meter of *Christabel* see *ibid.,* pp. 58–59n.; Ada L. F. Snell, "The Meter of Christabel," in *Fred Newton Scott Anniversary Papers* (Chicago, University of Chicago Press, 1929); Karl Shapiro, "English Prosody and Modern Poetry," *ELH,* XIV (1947), 77–92; Sir Herbert Read, *The True Voice of Feeling* (New York, Pantheon Books, 1953), pp. 27–28. See also George Whalley, "Coleridge on Classical Prosody: An Unidentified Review of 1797," *Review of English Studies,* II (1951), 248–249; Charles I. Patterson, "An Unidentified Criticism by Coleridge Related to *Christabel,*" *Publications of the Modern Language Association,* LXVII (1952), 973–988.

[13] The conclusion to Part II seems to bear an intelligible relationship to what has gone before, whatever the immediate circumstances of its composition. Part II ends with a father's harshness to his child, the result of a tragic misunderstanding. The conclusion, which Coleridge had called a "very metaphysical account of fathers calling their children rogues, rascals, and little varlets," presents a pretended and humorous harshness, and accounts for it by the tentative hypothesis that in this fallen world most strong passions are evil and in

consequence the passion of love must borrow its vocabulary from its opposite:

> Perhaps 'tis pretty to force together
> Thoughts so all unlike each other;
> To mutter and mock a broken charm
> To dally with wrong that does no harm:
> Perhaps 'tis tender too and pretty
> At each wild word to feel within
> A sweet recoil of love and pity!
> And what, if in a world of sin
> (O sorrow and shame should this be true!)
> Such giddiness of heart and brain
> Comes seldom save from rage and pain,
> So talks as it's most used to do?

Coleridge seems about to go on, "But what if the father's rage and pain should be genuine, as is Sir Leoline's; as may happen in a world of sin whose fatal influence can bring about such estrangement as this? That would indeed be sorrow and shame." In other words, the conclusion would have reëmphasized the tragic breach in the father-child relationship. This interpretation is strengthened by the earlier use of "sorrow and shame" to describe Christabel's fallen state: Geraldine avows to her that

> Thou knowest to-night, and will know tomorrow,
> This mark of my shame, this seal of my sorrow;

and the conclusion to Part I laments,

> O sorrow and shame! Can this be she,
> The lady, who knelt at the old oak tree?

[14] "Good music never tires me, nor sends me to sleep. I feel physically refreshed and strengthened by it, as Milton says he did.

"I could write as good verse now as ever I did, if I were perfectly free from vexations, and were in the *ad libitum* hearing of fine music, which has a sensible effect in harmonizing my thoughts, and in animating, and, as it were, lubricating my inventive faculty. The reason of my not finishing Christabel is not that I don't know how to do it—for I have, as I always had, the whole plan entire from beginning to end in my mind; but I fear I could not carry on with equal success the execution of the idea, an extremely subtle and difficult one" (*Table Talk*, July 6, 1833). The association of music with *Christabel* is significant. In fact, the topic of *Christabel* seems to have arisen in connection with music, which Coleridge had previously been discussing, and from which he had gotten to Milton, then to his own poetry, and finally to *Christabel* specifically. See the entire entry for this date.

[15] See Read, *op. cit.*, pp. 27–28. In keeping with his customary exhilarating view of Coleridge and romanticism, Sir Herbert emphasizes irregularity in *Christabel:* "An examination of this measure shows that it is even more irregular than Coleridge had forewarned us in his Preface. At least, if we take lines like:

> Of the huge, broad-breasted, old oak tree

or

> On the topmost twig that looks up at the sky

it is difficult to scan them without allowing, in the first case six, in the second five, accents. In other cases it is difficult to discover more than three:

My sire is of a noble line

or

Is the night chilly and dark."

I am predisposed to argue against this interpretation as giving too little heed to the base of unity or regularity which Coleridge used as his point of departure. Read seems to be assuming a principle of absolute, invariable accentuation not intended by the poet. The lines may be scanned as follows to show a much higher degree of regularity, if it is assumed that accent does not depend upon quantity or upon ordinary stress entirely, but rather upon interrelationships within the line or possibly within the period. That is, a syllable that would ordinarily be accented may yield to a stronger accent in its vicinity:

Of the *huge*/broad-*breast*/ed *old*/oak *tree*
On the *top*/most *twig*/that looks *up*/at the *sky*
My *sire*/is *of*/a *no*/ble *line*
*Is* the *night*//*chil*ly/and *dark*?

Thus interpreted, each line has four accents.

[16] See Shapiro, *op. cit.*

[17] The extent of repetition in *Christabel,* too great to represent in the text of this essay, can hardly be recognized without wearisome listing. Without attempting to be definitive, I have noted ninety-nine instances of significant repetition. The count is a listing of the lines in which repetition occurs, and does not include repetition within single lines or repetition, such as internal rhyme, alliteration, assonance, or consonance, in elements smaller than a word.

[18] The following statements on meter bear upon Coleridge's presumed practice in *Christabel:* "To read Dryden, Pope, &c., you need only count syllables; but to read Donne you must measure *Time,* and discover the *Time* of each word by the sense of Passion" (*Coleridge on the Seventeenth Century,* ed. R. F. Brinkley [Durham, N.C., Duke University Press, 1955], pp. 519–520).

"In the Iambic Pentameter of the *Paradise Lost,* I assume fifteen breves as the total quantity of each line—this isochrony being the identity or element of sameness, the varying quality of the isochronous feet constituting the difference; and from that harmony or fine balance of the two opposite (N.B. *not* contrary) forces, viz., identity and difference, results the likeness; and again, this likeness (*quicquid simile est, non est idem*) [is] reducible to a law or principle and therefore anticipable, and, in fact, though perhaps unconsciously expected by the reader, or auditor, constitutes poetic metre. Each line is a metre—ex. gr., we should not say, that an hexameter is a line of six metres, but that it is a metre of six feet. But the harmonious relation of the metres to each other, the fine medium between division and continuity, distinction without disjunction, which a good reader expresses by a pause without a cadence, constitutes rhythm. And it is this harmonious opposition and balance of metre and rhythm, superadded to the former balance of the same in quantity with the difference in quality, the one belonging to the lines, the other to the paragraphs, that makes the peculiar charm, the *excellency,* of the Miltonic poesy. The Greek epic poets left rhythm to the orators. The metre all but precluded rhythm. But the ancients *sang* their poetry. Now for a nation who, like the English, have substituted *reading,* impassioned and tuneful reading, I grant, but still *reading,* for *recitative,* this counter-action, this interpenetration, as it were, of metre and rhythm is the dictate of a sound judgment and like all other excellencies in the fine arts, a postulate of common sense fulfilled by genius . . ." (*ibid.,* p. 580). Coleridge's assumption of a uniform quantity to each line, balanced by variety in the metrical feet, and the further balance of meter in the line with rhythm in the verse paragraph, has a strong likeness to what he said of the meter of *Christabel* in his Preface, to which the poem's system of paragraphs adds a further similarity.

Of Beaumont and Fletcher he remarks, "It is true that *Quantity,* an almost iron Law with the Greek, is in our language rather a subject for a peculiarly fine ear, than any law or even rule; but then we, instead of it have first, accent; 2ndly, emphasis; and lastly, retardation & acceleration of the Times of Syllables according to the meaning of the words, the passion that accompanies them, and even the character of the Person that uses them" (*Coleridge's Miscellaneous Criticism,* ed. T. M. Raysor [Cambridge, Harvard University Press, 1936], pp. 66–67). Of Massinger he writes: ". . . the rhythm and metre are incomparably good, and form the very model of dramatic versification, flexible and seeming to arise out of the passions, so that whenever a line sounds immetrical, the speaker may be certain he has recited it amiss, either that he has misplaced or misproportioned the emphasis, or neglected the acceleration or retardation of the voice in the pauses . . ." (Brinkley, *op. cit.,* p. 676).